D0230420

Bring Him Home

The Search for Ronan

ORLA
KELLY
PUBLISHING

Ciaran Baxter

To our late mother, Eileen, and our late father,
Philip, who taught us how to become a family.

Acknowledgements

Writing a book is more difficult than I ever thought, and more rewarding than I can ever have imagined.

None of this would have been possible without the constant guidance of Kim Arnold, who's assistance and patience helped me to eventually finish this book.

I, and the Baxter family, will be forever eternally grateful to my long term friend, Tony Quilter, and the Garda Siochana and to Dermot Keating and the London Metropolitan Police, for all their efforts and advice in the search for Ronan. Both Tony and Dermot were our rocks of support, in what were the most extremely difficult times for the family.

I would also like to express special thanks to Ray Walker, Irish Press Attache of the Irish Embassy in London for his understanding and efforts. He saw two guys who were desperate to find their brother Ronan in the enormous city of London, and he dropped everything to help us.

To the Irish Press Association and all the Irish and London newspapers and television and radio editors and reporters, who kept Ronan's story on the front line, thank you.

We as a family would like to extend our sincere gratitude to all our friends, too many to name individually, who came to our side and helped at our time of need.

Finally, to my wife Sally, children Jamie, Lisa and Kayleigh who kept me going in those dark days and sustained me in times of doubt.

Go Raibh Maith Agat.

'For there is nothing lost, that may be found, if sought…' The Faerie Queene **Edmund Spencer**

Homelessness Statistics

Homelessness in Ireland 2018

- Peak official homelessness figure of 9968 (November 2018).
- Approximately one third under the age of 18.
- Some 40-50 homeless people died on the streets of Ireland.

  (Irish Times, 2018; Focus, Ireland, 2018; Peter McVerry Trust, 2018)

Homelessness in the UK 2018

- Official homelessness figure estimated at 320,000
- Approximately one half under the age of 18.
- Some 440 homeless people died on the streets of England and Wales.

  (BBC, 2018)

Homelessness in London 2018

- Official homelessness figure estimated at approximately 3000

- Number of homelessness-related deaths unknown.

(BBC, 2018)

Mental Health in Ireland

- Ireland has one of the highest rates of mental health illness in Europe.

- In 2016, some 18.5 per cent of the Irish population was recorded as suffering a mental health disorder such as anxiety, bipolar, schizophrenia, depression, or alcohol or drug use.

- Rates of depression recorded in Ireland were also well above the European average for both men and women.

(*Health at a Glance Report*, in The Irish Times, 24:02:19)

Schizophrenia in Ireland

Schizophrenia is a common serious mental health condition. While its exact cause is unknown, most experts believe that it is caused by a combination of genetic and environmental factors.

- Men and women are equally affected.
- In men, onset is usually between the ages of 15 and 30.
- In women, onset is usually later, between the ages of 25 and 30.
- There are about 3900 people currently living with the condition in Ireland.

Psychological symptoms include:

- hallucinations: hearing or seeing things that do not exist
- delusions: unusual beliefs that are not based on reality and often contradict the evidence
- muddled thoughts based on the hallucinations or delusions
- changes in behaviour
  (https://www.hse.ie/eng/health/az/s/schizophrenia, 24:02:19)

Contents

Part One

August 14th

"Ronan's missing."

It was my father ringing from the family home in Cork. No greeting. Straight to the point.

"He left the house yesterday afternoon, and he's just gone. I rang the hospital last night, and he never went back."

I was rooted to the spot. Frozen. Despite the bright Sunday morning sun shining down on Dundalk train station. Words died in my throat. I glanced at my watch, my mind racing. Eleven on the button. It would take at least five hours to get home. Maybe more on a Sunday. *Oh, God…*

"Ciaran? Hello? *Hello…!*"

The panic in Dad's voice jolted me back.

"Sorry. Yeah, I'm here, Dad. Look, you know Ronan. He'll be grand. You worry too much. He likes his home comforts too much to stay away for long. I'm sure he'll be back today or tomorrow at the latest. Probably just went off to Dublin or something. I'm on my way, Dad. It'll be ok."

After a few more words of reassurance to my father, I ended the call, and stood stock still amidst the hustle and bustle of the crowded station. I needed to gather myself. Three minutes earlier I'd been relaxed and happy, heading home after a lovely weekend away with my wife and children. Now busy, purposeful people rushed past me in their bright summer outfits, some accidentally barging into me – the only motionless person on the concourse. A couple of cheerful young backpackers had me spotted and headed toward me, their entire faces like open smiling question marks. No doubt they just needed directions or whatever. But as they got nearer, a certain tightness in my stance and around my mouth, made them abruptly veer away towards a sweet elderly couple who were sitting on a bench happily watching the world go by and enjoying a Cornetto.

The tannoy blared out its usual indistinct announcements, and the acrid smell of burnt coffee beans hit the back of my throat. The hiccupping wail of an angry toddler was drowned out by the rippling slams of train doors and the shriek of the guard's whistle. A train slowly pulled away from Platform 2, and in the brief silent aftermath, I gave way to a sinking feeling of pure dread, of foreboding. My brother Ronan, a particularly vulnerable and defenceless man, was missing. Despite everything I'd just said, I knew Dad wasn't overreacting.

This was bad.

Very bad.

Myself, my wife Sally, my kids Jamie, Lisa and Kayleigh, and Jamie's friend, Jack, were on our way home from Castleblayney after visiting our good friends, Dermot and Sinead. We'd met them on holiday in Spain a few years earlier, got on like a house on fire, and thanks to Sally, who is great at phoning and texting, had kept in touch. So a bit the worst for wear, I was still feeling great after a weekend of pure Monaghan craic. Now, as I considered the possible consequences of Ronan's disappearance, all that was nullified.

Looking around, I saw Lisa and Kayleigh joking and fooling around on the platform. No sign of the boys. Our train was due at eleven-twenty, meaning we'd arrive into Cork around four that afternoon. All being well, we could go straight to Dad's.

Five hours…Jesus!

With a brisk nod over at Sally, I stomped off down the platform in search of the lads. As usual, they were laughing and carefree, just leaning against a barrier at the end of the platform, watching out for the next train. When I barked at them to return to the rest of our family immediately, Jack looked really upset. At that moment, I couldn't have explained, maybe didn't even realise, that my uncharacteristic gruffness sprang from a heightened sense of protectiveness towards those I loved.

Our train journey home was muted. Cork were playing Clare in the quarter-final of the All-Ireland Hurling Championship, and I distracted myself from my dark thoughts by listening to the first half on Lisa's portable radio as the train hurtled south through the green summer countryside.

Once back in Cork we drove straight to my father's house and our home in Bishopstown where I was in time to watch the second half of the match on TV and attempted to keep my increasingly anxious dad on an even keel.

Talking through possible explanations, we came to the conclusion that Ronan must have gone off to Dublin for the weekend, or maybe for a few days' holiday somewhere. He had a bus pass which enabled him to travel freely and independently anywhere in Ireland. He had a few euro. And as he hadn't taken any time for himself over the last few months, we persuaded ourselves that he had simply needed a change of scene for a few days.

The only really strange aspect was that he had not told my father where he was going and simply walked out the front door the previous afternoon. Odd. But after all, Ronan was a grown man. While it may have been a bit inconsiderate to worry Dad, he did not have to account to us for his every movement or action. Sitting around my father's kitchen table, talking it through, seemed to give us a bit more perspective. It was just a glitch, a storm in a teacup. We drank our tea and told ourselves that he would return safe and sound in his own good time. And I headed for home with Sally and my children with a sense of relief.

But as I drifted into an uneasy sleep that night, all my worst fears came flooding back.

And I felt a nightmare nudging at the edges of my mind.

August 15th – 18th

The following couple of days dragged by, leaden and taut as the calm before a storm. Work became increasingly difficult to cope with as my concentration wandered and thoughts lay elsewhere. Fretful and exhausted, at times even angry, the premonition of loss was a low and constant hum in my mind.

As a family, we were resigned to waiting it out and clung to the idea that Ronan had travelled to Dublin and would return home to us before we knew it. We told ourselves, and each other, to be patient and understanding. But perhaps because Ronan had lived with Dad in the family house for the preceding seventeen years and he was the most familiar with his son's moods and habits, he eventually found Ronan's unexplained absence disturbing enough to report him missing to the local Bishopstown Gardaí on the evening of the Sunday. He stressed that Ronan was a vulnerable man with a history of mental health issues, that he was last seen at three in the afternoon, and that he had not returned to Cork University Hospital overnight as expected.

By now we had worked out that Ronan had left with his AIB Bank Deposit book and some cash - somewhere between five hundred and a thousand euro.

He had also taken his Bus Pass.

At that time, my father, Philip Baxter, was an extremely fit and mentally astute eighty-two year old man. Originally from Cavan, he had moved to Cork as a young man, courted and married a local girl named Eileen Hartnett, and eventually settled down in the newly developing suburb of Bishopstown. Seven Baxter children arrived in due course: Martin, the eldest son, with myself, Ciaran next; followed by Aidan, Brian and Ronan; with the two youngest, Maria and Joey, bringing up the rear. Dad was upstanding and strict, an old-school disciplinarian, who worked hard and provided well for his family. He held down a good job in industry and worked his way up through the ranks to become General Manager of Lucas Industries in Cork. He took early retirement in

1982, just two years after the untimely death of our mother.

In later years Dad proved to an involved and supportive parent, but I know he'd agree that Mum was the special one. The loving one. I can see her now; a kind, pretty, happy-go-lucky woman who lived for her children and loved socialising with friends and family.

Giver of Hugs.

Queen of the Lemon-meringue Pie.

Throughout the two long years of her battle with breast cancer, she somehow maintained her humour, dignity and pride. Her *self*.

Her tragic death on December 20th 1980, and funeral on Christmas Eve has left an indelible mark of sorrow on us all to this day. But it also gave us something more.

Directly after her funeral, my dad assembled his young family, and handed each of us a sealed envelope. Each one contained a special personalised letter written by Mum setting down her last thoughts and wishes for us, and her final assurances that she would look over us forever.

Like all large families, she understood we had our favourites and our fights. But every letter encouraged us, instructed us really, to look after each other in her place.

Always.

No matter what.

The Baxters must stand together.

The posthumous hopes of our wonderful, brave Mum, so hard for us to absorb in the depths of our shock and grief, have stayed with us all our lives, and turned out to be the foundation of the Baxter determination and strength on which our relentless search for Ronan was built.

August 19th – 20th

By Friday of that first week, the anticipation of Ronan's imminent return was building. For some reason I can't put into words, there was a tacit feeling amongst the family that a week was the longest he would reasonably stay away without a word. When he still hadn't turned up or contacted Dad by Saturday, the collective tension was at breaking-point and our composure began to crumble. We'd hit a wall. By now, the foreboding hum in my head was starting to bang.

Over the week, Dad had nearly killed himself visiting countless friends and acquaintances in person and making unending phone calls in the hope of hearing something, anything at all, about Ronan's whereabouts. It was hard to witness his increasing desperation for news. But nothing was forthcoming. No one had seen or heard a thing. It was as if Ronan had disappeared into thin air. At this stage, Dad had even abandoned taking his faithful dogs for their daily walk - the unbroken habit of a lifetime. He, and he alone would be the one to welcome Ronan home when he finally walked through the front door.

Although he was a thirty-nine year old man, Ronan had suffered from chronic depression for the previous fifteen years or so and was an habitual patient of Cork University Hospital. Even so, he took medications for his illness and enjoyed a reasonably 'normal' life with my father in the family home. Ronan was a man of many comforts. He revelled in his music and watching his favourite TV shows. He smoked far too many Benson & Hedges cigarettes for his own good.

While he didn't have a wide circle of friends, he was deeply loved by the entire Baxter clan and seemed quite happy and at peace with his situation. As a family, we had arranged to convert the garage adjoining the family home into to an independent flat in the event of anything happening to Dad in the future, Ronan could live on in the flat and the main house could be let to provide Ronan with financial independence.

He received a monthly disability cheque of about five hundred pounds from the UK Social Welfare office as he had briefly lived and worked in London when he was young. On top of that, Ronan also received a smaller weekly disability cheque of around twenty euro from the Irish Social Welfare. Living at home with very few expenses, this income was more than sufficient to meet his modest financial needs.

Earlier that summer, both Dad and the wider family noticed a clear deterioration in Ronan's mental condition. We all knew the signs only too well and could see that a black depression was taking hold. Successive consultations with doctors finally resulted in the decision to start Ronan on a new medication regime. Based on all the professional advice and information available, the new drug, Clozapine, promised substantial improvements in Ronan's condition.

So in June, following lengthy negotiations with Ronan, he was admitted to Cork University Hospital as an in-patient to begin the new course of treatment and to enable his doctors to monitor his progress and reactions to the medication. By all accounts, this was the standard medical procedure whenever this type of new medication was to be administered.

By July the hospital was sufficiently happy with Ronan's progress to recommend that he be discharged and attend on a daily out-patient basis. The whole family and my father in particular, were not convinced this would work out and insisted that the full new medical course be completed before Ronan would be released. A compromise was struck. Ronan would be free to leave the ward each morning, spend the day and evening at home, and return to the ward every night. As the hospital was only a ten or fifteen minute walk from the family home in Bishopstown, he could stroll back sometime between eight and nine each evening. It seemed an ideal solution. In fact, Ronan's life had been moving along well and we'd all felt optimistic that he'd turned the corner in his current depressive episode.

As a family, we had always ensured that his well-being was a priority, and his present, and even future comfort, health and financial security, had been well planned out and provided for. Looking back now, I think that's why we were so sure that after a week or so away from home, Ronan would be unable to resist coming back to enjoy the company, comforts and security he loved.

When Monday morning came round with no word from Ronan, our worst fears were realised. And as our belief in his return plummeted, a sense of unspoken dread rose up in its place. That little hum in my head, my gut reaction when Dad had rung me in Dundalk, had been right all along.

This was bad.

And I didn't know how to fix it.

With Ronan's continued absence constantly pulling at my thoughts, every second of the next few days dragged by in slow motion. Each minute, each hour, I prayed that Ronan would come home. Every time my phone rang, I grabbed it - sure it would be good news. And, of course, it wasn't. These brief bright moments followed by crashing hopelessness, my dad's dejection, and the increasing despair of the whole family, made it impossible for me to think about anything else. Our anguish grew palpable. There was no rest to be had at night and each day brought nothing but a growing sense of anxiety.

Yet despite our mutual distress, perhaps because of it, the family somehow managed to pull it together. We realised we couldn't just wait around any longer. We had to *do* something or we'd go mad.

The Baxters must stand together.

With Mum's words of love and support in our hearts, we calmed ourselves and made plans to approach the problem of tracking Ronan down as logically and systematically as possible.

A phone call to the Passport Office confirmed that, as we thought, Ronan did not hold a valid passport. This at least reassured us that he was still in the country. He had to be. He simply couldn't leave. So, having put together a list of the necessary contact details, each family member took part in the daunting task of ringing every hospital, hotel and hostel in Cork and Dublin for news or sightings of Ronan. While his CIE Bus Pass was valid for travel all over Ireland, and even Northern Ireland, we felt sure these two large anonymous cities were our best starting point. More worryingly, we now knew for sure that our brother had no more than a few hundred euro on him when he'd left home more than a week before.

As with the passport, we were all pretty sure that Ronan didn't own a mobile phone. But to be on the safe side, we contacted all the usual providers who confirmed this was still the case. Following a special request to obtain Ronan's bank account details and transactions, the AIB supplied a statement which showed that the last withdrawal from Ronan's account had been made on July 20th, leaving a healthy untouched balance of a thousand euro or so.

My brother, Martin, and myself arranged to meet Ronan's doctor in Cork University Hospital. She knew Ronan very well, having been his consultant since 2001, and once again walked us through his diagnosis of paranoid schizophrenia and chronic depression. While supportive and sympathetic, she was also direct and unequivocal, warning us that patients who abruptly stop taking Clozapine were likely to become extremely and rapidly unwell. Her blunt prognosis was deeply troubling, and our underlying anger and frustration towards both the medical team and ourselves began to boil over. Why hadn't we insisted that Ronan stay in hospital until the transition to the new medication had been fully completed? But, at this stage, guilt and recriminations were an indulgence we couldn't afford, a waste of precious time. We needed to focus our energies on locating him. Now more than ever.

At our request, the consultant provided us with a formal letter detailing Ronan's diagnosis and authorising immediate treatment. It was the best she could do for us under the circumstances. The drive home from the hospital passed in silence as we both processed the fact that our brother had no medication with him, and we had only four to six weeks to find him.

And how were we going to break all this to our father?

The search widened. I stayed in constant touch with Dad and the rest of the family. The phone was never out of my hand. Every day we scoured the nearby vacant or derelict buildings and combed the local Bishopstown parks and woods. But there was nothing. Nothing. We were at our wits end - desperate for any sign at all, for just a glimpse, a single clue.

Even though it had never once occurred to me that Ronan might harm himself, the doctor's recent discussion of schizophrenic symptoms played on my mind, and I could no longer ignore the terrifying possibility of suicide. These fears threatened to overtake me. So much so, that each day I had to psyche myself up, to fortify myself against what we might find. And each exhausting, fruitless search brought its own uneasy sense of relief.

Never a religious man, now I found myself imploring the gods, brokering deals, making promises to divinities I barely believed in, if only Ronan could be delivered back to us safe and well. All day, every day, of that first week, I literally prayed for news that Ronan had returned, or at least was safe.

Please God, just let him walk back in the same door he left through.

It was useless, of course. Every email, phone call and search drew a complete blank. I had never felt so drained in my life, yet sleep refused to come. Even through the sadness of Mum's final days, we had the comfort of knowing she was safe, that she wasn't alone or suffering. She was never *lost*.

As I lay there next to Sally in the darkness, my exhausted mind refused to be still, churning over and over, trying to dredge up some forgotten idea of where he could have gone.

Where could he be?

What was I missing?

I couldn't accept that Ronan might not be alive and yet I struggled to block out thoughts of suicide. On top of this, I was worried about the toll on Dad's health. He was eighty-two. This could be the end of him…

A sharp strip of dawn sunlight forced its way under the heavy bedroom curtains. Barely quarter to five on a Sunday morning. But getting up was a relief. Had it really only been a week since I'd sipped coffee on a sunny railway platform with nothing but a slight hangover and bickering kids to worry me? So much had happened in seven days. To my family. To my dad. To me. God knows, my emotions were all over the place.

For the first time, I found myself wondering not just where Ronan had gone, but why?

Was it purely the nature of his illness, a reaction to the new meds? Or had something happened in the hospital? Perhaps he was sad? Lonely? In trying so hard to care for him, had we made him feel like a child? Was he fed up of being the 'sick' brother, the 'problem' of the family? Maybe he had a secret friend, a relationship we didn't know about? Worst of all, was he deliberately hiding from us?

I'd always loved my brother very much, and the older I got, the more tolerant, the more deeply protective I felt towards him. But in that moment I realised I didn't know everything about him.

All I knew for certain was that it was now August 21st. Ronan had been missing for eight days. We had exhausted every method we could think of to trace him, and the longer this situation went on, the harder it would be us, for Dad. And the more disastrous it could be for Ronan.

The clock was ticking, and my fear was real.

I felt the wetness of tears on my face, and the panic rose up and lodged in my throat.

Ronan! Where are *you?*

August 21ˢᵗ

It went without saying that whatever it took, we would leave no stone unturned in our search for Ronan. That was a given. But at the same time, the situation was completely outside our experience. We just weren't sure where to turn next. We all felt we had to do, wanted to do, more. But what? It seemed impossible. We decided to put our heads together and hold a family gathering in Dad's house in Bishopstown on the Sunday to thrash out a course of action. Something practical. Realistic. We figured that a coordinated approach would not only ensure that everyone was completely on board, but more importantly, would safeguard against the needless duplication of individual efforts. It would help to keep track of everything and make sure all possibilities were followed through.

Everyone turned up for one on the dot as arranged, their expectant faces taut with weariness and dark unspoken fears.

At the time of Ronan's disappearance, mental health issues were considered taboo in Ireland, and to a certain extent, they still are. It's unclear why this should be, considering just how many people cope with and live their lives day-in and day-out with these problems, not to mention the partners and immediate or extended family members affected by the mental health difficulties of their loved ones.

A million miles away from the Victorian images of incarcerated lunatics, 'out of sight-out of mind' for their own good and everyone else's, in reality the most commonly diagnosed forms of mental health illnesses are depression, paranoia and anxiety. Body-dysmorphia manifested by the eating disorders anorexia and bulimia largely afflicts young girls and women. Schizophrenia is worryingly prevalent in young men.

If we're honest, in this day and age, anyone who hasn't been touched by some form of mental health issue is very lucky - and very rare. In fact, despite the lingering associations with the taint and shame of insanity, mental ill-health is ubiquitous in the twenty-first century. Literally all around us. And on the rise. Yet, much like ourselves, I guess most people still fear a social backlash and prefer to deal with this stuff as privately as they can: with the help of trusted friends and family, and the often inadequate medical support and state assistance available to them. Even these days - in the supposedly tolerant and inclusive 'new' Ireland.

A number of years ago, the very word *schizophrenia* was enough to set off the alarm bells of the mainstream population; a misunderstood skeleton you never wanted to come out of the closet. But at our family meeting that day, we were forced to concede that the details of Ronan's mental health issues could no longer remain an in-house private matter. In what seemed like a gross invasion of his privacy, we realised that to stand any chance of finding him, of helping him, we would have to cross the line and air Ronan's most intimate affairs in the public domain.

As usual, my amazing sisters Maria and Joey were ahead of the game and had already organised various photographs of Ronan, which it was agreed they would send to my late friend,

Declan O'Donovan. Declan, a graphic designer, kindly arranged to produce posters bearing a large image of Ronan and our contact information. To maximise their impact, they would be heavily bannered with the words 'Missing Person', laminated for protection against the unpredictable Irish weather, and displayed in as many public places throughout the city and county as we could think of.

Someone also remembered that our good friend, Derry O'Connor, worked for Bus Éireann and agreed to contact him to ask to look through the CCTV footage of the main Cork bus depot at Parnell Place for Saturday August 13th. We also set about identifying an Irish Rail contact to request permission to review their CCTV footage of Cork's Kent Station for the afternoon of the same day. Finally, we hit on contacting my long-standing friend Tony Quilter for help. As youngsters, Tony and myself had gone through UCC together, and on graduating, he had followed his late father's footsteps into the Garda Siochána. At the time Ronan went missing, he had risen through the ranks to Detective Superintendent. His advice and assistance could be a godsend.

Everyone there that day was so on edge, and it was inevitable that our discussions were occasionally heated and panic-stricken, even a little angry. But with the one shared objective, to find Ronan and bring him safely home, we ultimately managed to keep on track, make a plan, and divide up the various tasks in a logical and coherent way. Looking back, we were all so distraught and sleep-deprived by then, I don't know how we managed to string two words together. Love is a powerful force. Just having a plan made things seem more positive and the relentless tension was occasionally broken by the occasional light-hearted anecdote or joke about Ronan walking back in the door to join the meeting about his disappearance. My father sat there throughout, quiet but determined. He seemed to accept that at this point, we, his sons and daughters, had to take over.

So the wheels were now in some sort of motion. The tightness in my gut unclenched, and the hum in my head quietened a little for the first time in days.

Not for the first time, my thoughts swung back to Mum's final entreaty.

Always look after each other.

I closed my eyes, and there she stood before me.

We will, Mum. We will.

We had to bring Ronan home.

August 22nd

The same old smile and hearty handshake, the man stood in my father's doorway exuding a reassuring mixture of composure and compassion. In the hallway behind me, my father relaxed into his first smile in days and extended his hands in a gesture of welcome and gratitude. He clearly believed a saviour had arrived. It was just after midday on Monday, and as promised Detective Superintendent Tony Quilter, my old college pal and good friend had come to the family home to meet us.

Dad was old-school: a profoundly proud man who kept his own counsel and generally pushed on through life's problems as manfully as possible. Like many of us, he was inclined to mask potentially distressing or embarrassing situations with self-deprecation and humour, and as someone unaccustomed to sharing his private business and emotions, this first experience of revealing fear and vulnerability in relation to Ronan's disappearance beyond the immediate family circle was a huge hurdle for him. But Tony's calm manner and seasoned professionalism soon put any initial discomfort to rest.

I told him how Ronan had walked out the front door on that Saturday afternoon and how my dad had reported Ronan as missing on the following day. We gave a detailed description of the clothes he was wearing when we last saw him, and I filled him in on our family meeting of the previous day.

Tony recorded all the details and spent the remainder of his time with us asking numerous questions and taking further notes. He promised to look into the matter and get back to me within a day or so. His visit finished as it started; with a warm grin and a firm handshake.

During the day, my brothers Martin and Brian started trawling through the CCTV footage at Cork City Bus Station and Train Station which Derry had kindly organised for them. As agreed, we concentrated our review from three onwards on Saturday 13th August; the time Ronan had disappeared. Meantime, my other brother Aidan and sisters Maria and Joey spent the day sorting out the Missing Person posters. After collecting the rush-job from the printers, they set about pinning these up in shops, post offices, and everywhere and anywhere they could obtain permission to display them. Over the coming days and weeks, these posters would become part of us; carried and posted everywhere by all of us all of the time.

I stayed on with my dad after Tony left and yet again we wracked our brains to think where Ronan could have gone. At nine days missing we knew the situation was escalating and we were terrified. If he was still alive, he had no medication. Time was of the essence and we needed to find him. Soon.

We were in the midst of our speculations when two detectives from the local Bishopstown Garda Station arrived to talk myself and Dad about Ronan's case. We sat around the kitchen table, and their questions came thick and fast in an intense, and what at times felt like, an intrusive process. Once again the detectives took copious notes as we outlined Ronan's full history and the events of Saturday 13th and the steps the family had taken to find him to date. By the time the detectives eventually left around 6pm we were both emotionally drained. They thanked us and assured us that they would be in touch. The search for Ronan had now crossed the boundary from a private family issue into a matter of public record.

The wheels were now definitely in motion.

August 23rd – 26th

On the Tuesday and Wednesday, we continued to take turns trawling through the bus and train station CCTV footage of the week in question. Wading through the images of each of the numerous cameras was a tedious and time-consuming process - but we had no choice. Still, as each unsuccessful day went by, it was with tired eyes and an increasing sense of futility that my sisters Joey and Maria reviewed the train station footage while Martin, Brian and I concentrated our efforts on the bus station. Every frame from every camera had to be carefully scrutinised to as not to miss even the most fleeting glimpse of our brother.

Although we knew that Ronan had no passport, I had requested Tony Quilter's help in organising a review of the Cork Airport CCTV footage for the Saturday of Ronan's disappearance. We had established that the only flight from Cork to London on that day had departed at 4.15pm. I don't know why I arranged this exactly. I didn't expect anything to come of it; really it was just a box-ticking exercise. But Ronan had been drawn to London once before, so it was an 'all bases covered', 'every avenue explored' type of thing. More an intuition than a hope.

In any event, Tony was as good as his word and phoned me early on Tuesday morning with instructions to go through the Cork Airport CCTV with Gardaí that evening at 6pm.

While I was sincerely grateful for Tony's efforts on our behalf, it was with pretty low expectations that Martin and myself were met by the Airport Police at the Arrivals Hall and taken into the Cork Airport Security Office. Ronan had no passport. He *couldn't* actually leave the country...The bus and train station seemed a much more realistic option. But as we were there, we threw ourselves into the task and spent the rest of the evening and most of the night peering at images of the various airport areas covering the 12pm-6pm time-frame of Saturday 13th August.

At this stage we had also contacted the ferry companies operating out of Ringaskiddy Port on the outskirts of Cork City only to be told that

Ronan's name did not appear on the passenger lists of any ferry which sailed during the week commencing August 13th.

On Wednesday evening two representatives of the local Missing Persons Search and Recovery Organisation called to the family home. The entire Baxter family listened in silence as they spoke of their volunteer status, previous case experiences, and their willingness to organise and co-ordinate search missions in the local area and in the city areas, including searches of rivers and wooded areas. Echoing our own worst fears, they broached the possibility that Ronan was no longer alive at this time.

On leaving, we expressed our sincere thanks for their support and promised to stay in touch. We meant every word, but we were not ready to accept the idea that Ronan was not alive. It was unimaginable. I thought of Mum's enduring love for us. And Dad's anguish eating away at him. One way or another, we had to find him. Bring him home. *But how?*

Everywhere we looked, we turned up a blank. My hopes gave way to frustration and despair.

And anger. The whole thing was ridiculous! How *could* a grown man disappear off the face of the earth? And despite increasing conjectures to the contrary, I wouldn't, couldn't, entertain the notion that my brother was dead. My whole being rebelled against the idea. Finding Ronan became my all-consuming, my only conscious thought.

Meanwhile, the media swung into action. On Wednesday August 24th a news item from Bishopstown Garda Station appealing for information helping to find Ronan was broadcast on the national RTE News. Following this first public announcement, another Garda appeal appeared as a small news item in the Thursday edition of the Evening Echo local newspaper along with a further Garda appeal in the Cork Examiner of the same day. Tony Quilter also phoned me to say that he would call to the family home that morning and arrived with the same friendly grin and warm handshake. We took up our now war-cabinet position around the kitchen table.

My father looked tired and worn as Tony summarised the previous week's efforts culminating in no trace of Ronan. A consummate professional, Tony quickly got to the point: we would have to launch a full-scale media campaign, and the family would have to make the direct personal appeal for information. Tony assured us that a direct appeal to the public for help was vitally important to find out what happened to Ronan since all other efforts to date had failed.

As it was clear that Dad was too fragile to deal directly with the media, I volunteered to act as the Baxter family spokesperson. Tony went on to give us advice which ultimately was to prove invaluable in dealing with the media. Basically, it was my responsibility to use the media to achieve my objectives. Tony stressed the need to choose media outlets which best ensured maximum benefit in our quest to find Ronan. His warnings to steer clear of elements of the Press who distort and sensationalise such human interest stories as a means of boosting sales remained at the forefront of my mind throughout the entire ordeal.

Once Tony had our consent, he agreed to contact RTE News that evening, and he left with the assurance that he would be back to me the following morning. I felt myself break out in a cold sweat as the reality of Ronan's disappearance hit me anew. On top of that, I realised there was no going back now. Ronan was going to become *a story*, private Baxter family business was going to be held up for all to see, and I was the one charged with 'washing our dirty linen' in public.

Early on the Friday morning Pascal Sheehy of the RTE News rang to ask whether he could call to the family home that morning and within the hour later Dad's kitchen was ablaze with RTE lighting and jammed with camera and sounds crews. In a bit of a daze, I placed a few Missing Person posters of Ronan on the kitchen table before Dad and myself were directed to take our places opposite Pascal Sheehy. I had the surreal sensation of being in a soap opera, as a whole host of producers, directors, and technical crew readied themselves and called for silence to record the scene. Cameras finally rolling, the experienced RTE man then reiterated the main particulars of events and plied us with a number of questions. My nerves were jangling: the whole thing was so outside my comfort zone and yet it was vital that I perform well. Not only did I need to come across sympathetically and represent my father and entire family favourably, but I also needed to provide clear and accurate information about my brother.

Looking back now, the actual interview was a blur. I don't remember much about it. He asked the questions. I answered. I got through it and the media juggernaut was launched at full speed. Before Pascal and the RTE entourage left, I asked when our public appeal news item would appear, and was astonished that he intended to air it on the 1pm news that same day. Moreover, the appeal would be repeated on the 6pm evening news and once again on the 9pm main news on RTE1.

There was now no going back.

Once again, I stayed with my father for most of that day. My sister Joey also arrived, as did my brother, Martin. We huddled together to watch the RTE News on TV at 1pm and, unbelievably, there it was. About half way through the programme, maybe the third or fourth item, Pascal Sheehy appeared in our kitchen with my dad and I sitting at the kitchen table. He spoke of the background to Ronan's disappearance and finished with an appeal from the family for help in finding him. The same appeal would appear on the 6pm RTE news and the 9pm news.

Until that day, Ronan's issues with mental illness, his disappearance, and our family appeal were known locally but had not been national public knowledge. Not for the first time, I recalled my Mum's wonderful letters and took strength from her words. I prayed that our leap into the public domain was not an unnecessary betrayal of our brother's privacy and would help us to track him down.

As it turned out, the Baxter family phones rang off the hook that same afternoon. Even though we had posted Missing Person posters all over Cork City, the fact that the family appeal had warranted air time on TV seemed to galvanize numerous offers of help from relatives, neighbours, friends and even complete strangers. It was as if people now felt it was okay to contact us and talk about Ronan's disappearance.

During the day, Tony's words of advice popped into my head: 'Choose your media outlets to get the maximum exposure and benefit for Ronan'. At the same time, somewhere down the line, I'd heard of the Press Association and had some idea of its function. The two trains of thought seemed to spark off each other and give me an idea. I looked them up. Yep, the number was right there. On the spur of the moment, I decided to take a chance and ring them. *Nothing ventured…* And it was nothing short of a miracle that Barry happened to take my call that day.

As I launched into the broad strokes of Ronan's illness and disappearance I realised that he was extremely busy so I offered to send him on the complete details by email instead. I emphasised that I wasn't really offering him a story as such - Ronan's disappearance was already established in the public domain. No. What I was really looking for was his networking knowledge around Irish newspaper editors and reporters who could help me.

Barry explained this was not possible as that the Press Association does not deal directly with the public, but he did give me his email address and kindly offered to help in any way he could.

And true to his word, by Friday evening I received a list of email addresses and contact numbers of key media people in Ireland. By that evening, I had managed to send numerous emails and photographs of Ronan to the various newspaper editors in Ireland along with sincere thanks to Barry who maintained daily contact with me during the coming days and weeks. And so was born another key relationship which ended up guiding all my subsequent dealings with the media. Just when I'd thought we'd come to a complete impasse in our search, a sudden inspiration and a little leap of faith had moved me to make the right call to the right person at the right time. I felt my Mum's hand at work in this new avenue of hope, looking over us all, forever, as she'd vowed she would.

Later that evening, around half nine, I was slumped in the armchair at home. The evening TV news had just finished and Sally and the kids were as subdued as myself. We were all exhausted one way or another. When my phone rang again, it was all I could do to answer, but I saw it was my friend Ted and I knew he'd keep calling till he got hold of me. I answered only to be told that he'd be collecting me to go out for a drink in ten minutes. I tried to convince him that I was not up to it, but resistance was futile. That was that. And so, half an hour later, I found myself standing in my local, glass in hand, surrounded by the noisy throng letting rip at the end of the working week. The banality, *the absurdity*, of the situation struck me. I knew Ted meant well, but it wasn't as if going out for a drink could magically fix things... it was making me feel worse.

People who knew me, mostly caught my eye and nodded a greeting which I automatically returned. It felt utterly cold-hearted to be out socialising when Ronan was missing and could be at risk of homelessness, serious illness, or worse. These were the thoughts whirling around my mind. And if those were my own thoughts, I was too mortified to imagine what the locals and customers were thinking of me. By now I felt sure that most people in the bar had seen the broadcast about of Ronan's disappearance and our family's appeal earlier that day. And now here I was, just hours later, out for a bit of Friday night craic with my friends? No wonder nobody even mentioned Ronan. Of course, I may have been imagining it, wronging everyone, but I was bone tired and stressed. I felt conspicuous and trapped.

Abruptly I left my unfinished drink on the counter and muttering a quick 'see you' to Ted, barged through the crowded doorway and dived out into the clean night air. The sheer relief of the quiet! I now accepted there could be no rest, no distraction, no let-up of any kind, until Ronan was restored to us. I breathed in deeply and slowly exhaled. Welcomed the solitary stroll home and the chance to be alone to gather my thoughts on the traumatic events of the day just passed. My senses heightened, I took in the vaulted skies above me, the solid ground beneath my feet.

I can *do this.*

The insistent ringing of my mobile was like a violation of the quiet country road. Not again! 10.45. Tony. My heart was in my mouth as I answered. Maybe he had news .... He didn't. He'd just returned from Dublin and was ringing from the main Cork City Garda Station to check how things had gone with RTE. He had a few additional questions for me to answer too, but I sensed that his call was more about the family's well-being after today's events than about Ronan. I continued walking home as we went through everything and ended the call just as I got to my front door.

The house was silent. I went straight through to the kitchen and drank a glass of water at the sink, my pale worried face reflected ghost-like in the darkened window. Stealing upstairs, I peeped in and gulped down the innocent musty smell of my sleeping kids – dewy skin, outflung limbs, fluttering eyelids - envying their carefree dreams. And naturally enough, I suppose, my thoughts drifted to how I'd feel, how I'd cope, if suddenly, inexplicably, they were gone. But I couldn't imagine it. It was unbearable even to try.

My poor father.

If anything happens to Ronan, it could be the end of Dad…

And without Dad we'll lose our last link to Mum…

We'll be lost too...we'll be orphans...

I knew I was spiralling. The stress of the last ten days finally swallowing me, pulling me down. The whole thing was useless - a stupid, futile, wild goose-chase. I just wanted to lie down and sleep.

For a year.

I'M. SO. TIRED.

And then I thought of Mum, lying in her hospital bed. Bravely confronting the end, and in the face of those insurmountable odds, pouring all her energy into those letters in a final surge of hope and love. Well, if she could keep going, we could. I could. My own children were safe and well, thank God. For the time being, I would have to entrust them to their mother's care, because from here on in, my entire focus would have to be finding Ronan.

Decision made, I crept along the landing, and undressed quietly in the family bathroom. Went to the loo, brushed my teeth - the usual. In the hushed stillness of my bedroom, I could hear the familiar rhythms of Sally's deep REM sleep. But as I inched under the covers, she instinctively reached for me and held me close to her all night as I lay there counting down the minutes till the dawn.

August 27th – 29th

The national newspapers on both Saturday and Sunday of that weekend carried various news stories appealing for information about Ronan. Nearly all included a photograph of Ronan which was essential from the point of view of public sightings and recognition. While I continued to keep Barry of the Press Association updated with any developments, I felt raw and exposed by the unfamiliar glare of publicity. I'm sure the whole family felt the same.

Night turned to day, and day turned to sleepless night as that excruciating weekend dragged by. On Monday August 29th major news articles and photographs of Ronan were carried in the Irish Examiner and the Irish Independent newspapers. That morning I was interviewed by Ann Murphy, a reporter with the Evening Echo which also featured a major news article and photograph of Ronan that evening. The article reiterated that the family had examined CCTV footage of the bus and train station in the city as well as at Cork

Airport, and went on to report that Ronan was unlikely to have left the country since he did not hold a valid passport.

And then, out of the blue, that Monday evening, came the very first breakthrough.

Tony Quilter rang around 7.30 to inform us that a man from Bishopstown had spotted Ronan at Cork Airport at around 7.30pm on Saturday 13th August. He was absolutely positive of the date and time as he and his family had been getting a holiday flight and he had noticed Ronan standing at the entrance to the Departure Area as they went through to the boarding gate. Moreover, the man identified the exact spot beside a supporting column at the Departures entrance where he saw Ronan.

On returning from two weeks holiday on Saturday 27th he had seen Ronan's photograph and the news article on the Evening Echo on the Monday afternoon and immediately phoned Bishopstown Garda Station.

Tony asked that I meet him at the airport in half an hour. I phoned my brother Martin en route and we both arrived to meet Tony. The Gardaí were clearly puzzled by the call. So were we. Why was Ronan in Cork Airport when he had no passport and the only flight that he might have taken to London had left almost three hours earlier? It didn't make any sense.

Tony suggested Martin and myself grab a coffee while he reviewed the Saturday 13th CCTV footage for the location specified by the witness. We waited on tenterhooks.

Tony returned within the hour. It *was* Ronan at the departures gate at 7.30pm that evening. Apparently the 4.15pm flight to London that day had been delayed and did not depart until 8pm that evening. One mystery solved. We had previously looked at CCTV footage up to 6pm that evening. Nobody had told us that the flight to London had been delayed. So it was now all but definite: Ronan had flown to London. Tony was absolutely incensed. Ronan didn't even have a passport; he had a *Bus Pass*, for God's sake…He demanded a copy of the passenger list from Aer Lingus to be made available by the following day.

We would finally know for sure whether Ronan had indeed flown to London on that fateful day.

The confirmation that Ronan had flown to London resulted in conflicting emotions: hope and despair. Our immediate overwhelming relief that Ronan had not committed suicide soon gave way to the realisation that we still didn't know why he had gone or where he was. More than two weeks had been wasted searching for him in Ireland and he was now most likely alone in London without his medication, without a passport to get home. The money in his bank account remained untouched.

It was all too clear we had merely substituted one search for another.

And we were now looking for a needle in one of the biggest haystacks in the world.

London.

Nine million inhabitants.

Vast.

Sprawling.

Anonymising.

We would need another miracle.

August 30th – 31st

By the following mid-day, the Gardaí categorically confirmed that Ronan had flown to London on August 13th, yet earlier that morning the Evening Echo had contacted me for confirmation that Ronan had been identified via Cork Airport CCTV footage. As I hadn't known for sure myself and had not yet contacted Barry at the Press Association, the speed at which this development had been leaked to the media stunned me. In any event, that afternoon the Evening Echo carried another major news article on Page 2: Ronan's story was edging closer to the front page with each passing day.

In the article, I took the opportunity to thank the Gardaí, the media, and the public for their support and help, but emphasised the increasing urgency of finding him as he was now more than two weeks without his medication. The article concluded by reporting that our search was moving across the water to totally unknown territory.

These were no idle words. It was completely foreign territory to us and the scale of the new task before us was daunting. One of my favourite business maxims "Fail to Prepare, Prepare to Fail" rang in my ears. It was clear to me that our only chance at all of tracing Ronan in London was to harness the assistance of as many media outlets, humanitarian agencies, missing person organisations and police departments as humanly possible.

We held another family meeting in my dad's house on Tuesday night to touch base with each and formulate a logical plan that we all agreed on. Despite the bustle of full attendance, the initial euphoria of the sighting in Cork Airport had died away and the overall mood was sombre. My dad did his usual and tried to lift our spirits but there was now a real sense of frustration and anxiety. Everyone agreed to connect with as many links and contacts in London as they could, and it was agreed that Martin and I would fly to London to carry on the search on Saturday September 3rd, leaving just Wednesday to Friday of that week to prepare and organise our strategy.

On Wednesday 31st August I got in touch with Ann Murphy and on that afternoon the *Evening Echo* headlined with a photograph of Ronan and an appeal for details of any media contacts in London. The article covered the full front page and included a family photograph of my dad, my wife Sally, my sister Maria with her six week old son, two of my children, Lisa and Kayleigh, and myself. The copy explained that we needed to establish the right channels before we left as we wanted to set up a big media campaign in London. We needed urgent help.

So Ronan was finally front page news. We had passed the point of comfort and concern for our own privacy. We would do whatever it would take to find Ronan. On Thursday I phoned Barry in the Press Association, promising him an email with a full update of developments and pleaded with him for a name and reference for the London Office of the UK Press Association.

The poor man protested that he should not even be talking to me, never mind sending me contact details or helping me. I knew this was true. So I made a pact with him. I solemnly promised that when I found Ronan – and I fully intended to find him - I would give Barry an exclusive on the story of his recovery. He would be the first and only journalist we would revert to.

To be honest, he must have figured this would never happen because it seemed unlikely that we would find Ronan at this stage, but as a decent guy he relented and agreed to provide me with a reference and a name in the London Press Association. He also promised to forward his media contact details for the greater London area.

The overseas search was up and running.

During that two day period, the whole family dived into researching phone numbers and addresses for the London Missing Persons Association, the Salvation Army, the London Red Cross and other organisations and bodies which we thought would help. I prepared and sent out an initial Press Release for the UK media outlining Ronan's need for medication and enclosing a photograph of Ronan.

The list of media sources and humanitarian organisations which received the initial UK Press Release was endless. It included the

Metro Free Sheet, the UK National Missing Persons Organisation, The London Evening Standard, Romford Recorder, The Big Issue, The Ilford Recorder, The Daily Mail, The London Independent, The Guardian, The London Times, RTE London, BBC Local TV, BBC London. The list went on and on. It included every newspaper circulated and every humanitarian organisation in the London area. We also sent the initial Press Release to every TV station in the London area including the popular BBC TV programme, *CrimeWatch*.

The contact details for all the London media and humanitarian organisations came in from all different sources, enabling me to start building the comprehensive database of London contacts which would prove invaluable in the days ahead.

That week we basically blitzed the London media with Ronan's Press Release, the thrust of which was that Ronan needed to be located urgently to get his medication to him and arrange for immediate medical attention. Our enquiries had determined that there were thousands and thousands of "missing" people in London. Those were people who did not want to be found and were happy to remain anonymous for whatever reason. If we were to have any chance of finding Ronan, we believed the best way forward was to appeal for help in finding him so that we could simply get his necessary medication to him.

By now the local newspaper, the Evening Echo, and its reporter Ann Murphy, were in daily contact with me. I was aware that the Echo had an associated newspaper in London called the Irish Post and I had managed to persuade Ann to organise a reference and a contact for me with the Irish Post in London. She put me in contact with the editor, a guy called Frank Murphy, and a meeting was set up for early the following week in London.

Amidst all the turmoil on Thursday morning of that week, our good friend and neighbour Barry Coffey arrived at my front door bearing a huge platter of freshly-made sandwiches. It transpired that after seeing our family appeal for help, he had phoned his good friend Dermot Keating of Scotland Yard in London.

Dermot, originally from County Kerry, had emigrated to London years earlier and had joined the London Police. In a glittering career, he had risen through the ranks to become Detective Chief Inspector at Scotland Yard. This was a fantastic plus from our point of view. A high-ranking police official in the very heart of London's premier police force – it was a sign.

Barry phoned Dermot from my kitchen that morning and, having introduced me, left me to outline Ronan's situation. We agreed to keep in touch during the day and Dermot promised to arrange a meeting in Scotland Yard with the London Police Missing Persons Division for Monday 5th September. He would come back to me the following day with the arrangements.

That Thursday afternoon I phoned Tony Quilter to update him on our preparations. Wouldn't you know it; Tony had worked on a number of UK/Ireland joint police operations in recent times and knew Dermot well. He agreed to phone Dermot that evening and give him a full heads-up on Ronan's case to date. Another key link in the search for Ronan in London had been forged. It looked like our luck was turning.

We were beginning to break through the Chinese walls.

The family had arranged for a final meeting in the family home on the Friday evening to exchange information and double-check that everything that could be done before we travelled had been done. I arrived in good time because I wanted to catch Dad alone. I was becoming extremely concerned about the effect all the media coverage was having on him. As we sat together at the now infamous Baxter kitchen table, drinking tea and reflecting on the events of the hectic week just passed, Dad looked more tired and dispirited than I'd ever seen him - even when Mum was dying. One of those uncanny moments of silence fell between us and I knew something was coming. Then he pulled himself up, looked me straight in the eye, and spoke the words that tore into my heart.

"Bring him home, Ciaran. Bring him home. Dead or alive."

Photographs Part One

Mum and Dad on their Wedding Day 1957

Early photo of some of the Baxter siblings

Lucas Industries, Bachelors Quay, Cork where Dad worked

Weekend watch: holiday feelin

Family appeals for help over missing man

by Olivia Kelleher

THE family of a Corkman who has been missing for two weeks yesterday issued an emotional appeal for information leading to his safe return.

Ronan Baxter, 39, disappeared from his home near Curraheen in Bishopstown in Cork city at 4.30pm on Saturday August 13th and hasn't been seen since.

His brother Kieran said yesterday that he was 'absolutely demented' with worry about his missing brother who is the third youngest in a family of seven.

"Ronan lived at home in Bishopstown with my father so it has been really hard on him. We are so worried. We have explored every option even checking CCTV cameras at the train and bus stations and we haven't spotted him. He wasn't driving a car so the only thing we know is that he must be getting around by train or bus. It defies logic. He just seems to have vanished into thin air."

Posters of Ronan Baxter have been placed at bus shelters throughout Cork city and gardaí asked GAA fans who travelled to Dublin yesterday for the Cork-Kerry match to be vigilant for any sighting of the 39-year-old.

The Baxters initially believed that Ronan may have travelled to Dublin for the weekend but became anxious when he failed to return.

He left the house with a small amount of cash and his bank book but he has failed to make any

Ronan Baxter: 39-year-old has been missing for two weeks.

withdrawals to date. The missing man doesn't have a valid passport so gardaí believe he is probably still in this country.

Kieran Baxter says he has become increasingly concerned for Ronan over the last few days as he must be running low on cash.

"You would expect to see a withdrawal at this stage. He had some money with him but not a whole lot. We would be asking people to look out for him. He can't just have vanished without someone seeing him."

Mr Baxter is 5ft 11in tall with brown hair, a heavy set frame and blue eyes. When last seen he was wearing a grey coat, black tracksuit and runners. Ronan generally wears distinctive gold framed glasses but he didn't have them with him on the day he went missing.

Anyone with information is asked to contact the Gardaí in Bishopstown in Cork on 021-4541012.

BUSYTODAY

Irish Examiner newspaper appeal

Irish Independent
Monday, 29 August, 2005

Missing man's family issue emotional appeal for help

Olivia Kelleher

THE family of a man who has been missing for two weeks yesterday issued an emotional appeal for information leading to his safe return.

Ronan Baxter (39) disappeared from his home near Curraheen, Bishopstown, Cork city, at 4.30pm on August 13 and hasn't been seen since.

His brother Kieran said yesterday that he was "absolutely demented" with worry about his brother, who is the third youngest in a family of seven.

"Ronan lived at home in Bishopstown with my father so it has been really hard on him. We are so worried. We have explored every option even checking CCTV cameras at the train and bus stations and we haven't spotted him. He wasn't driving a car so the only thing we know is that he must be getting around

by train or bus. It defies login. He just seems to have vanished in to thin air."

Posters of Ronan Baxter have been placed at bus shelters throughout Cork city. Meanwhile, gardaí asked GAA fans who travelled to Dublin yesterday for the Cork/Kerry match to look out for the 39-year-old.

The Baxters initially believed that Ronan may have travelled to Dublin for the weekend but became anxious when he failed to return. He left the house with a small amount of cash and his bank book but he has failed to make any withdrawals to date. The missing man doesn't have a valid passport so he probably still in the country. Kieran Baxter says he has become increasingly concerned for Ronan over the last few days as he must be running low on cash.

You would expect to see a withdrawal at this stage. He had some money with him but not a whole lot. We would be asking people to look out for him. He can't just have vanished without someone seeing him."

Mr Baxter is 5ft 11' tall with brown hair, a heavy set frame and blue eyes. When last seen he was wearing a grey coat, black tracksuit and runners. He wears gold-rimmed glasses but didn't have them with him when he went missing. Anyone with information is asked to contact gardaí in Bishopstown, Co Cork on 021-4543012.

Ronan Baxter ... disappeared from his home near Bishopstown on August 13 and hasn't been seen since.

MORE EUROPE
LESS EURO

Birmingham. Edinburgh. Glasgow.
Liverpool. London. Heathrow. Manchester.

€16

Communicating with UFOs 'is not science fiction'

Irish Independent newspaper appeal

Page 2 **EVENING ECHO,** Monday, August 29, 2005 **ECHONEWS**

Family make plea to missing son

By ANN MURPHY
www.murphy@eecho.ie

THE family of a man missing for more than two weeks have appealed to him to contact them.

Roman Baxter, aged 29, pictured right, disappeared from his house in Berwithch, Bishopstown, on August 13.

He lives with his 62-year-old father Philip and his family believe that Mr Baxter is still alive.

"On behalf of my distressed father and the rest of my family, I am appealing to Roman to return home," said his concerned brother, Kieran.

"I am also appealing to anyone who has seen him to contact the gardaí to let us know where he is."

Kieran said that Roman had been suffering from depression for a number of years and was on medication.

The Baxter family believe that Roman is alive, because he took money and his bank book with him when he left his home of 4.30pm on August 13.

No money has yet been withdrawn from his bank account.

"He just walked out the door without saying anything to my father," said Kieran.

"He had not been fed well in the days before he left but we believe that was because he had made his mind up that he was going to go somewhere," he said.

The family have examined CC TV footage at the bus and train station in the city, as well as at Cork Airport.

But it is unlikely that Roman Baxter has left the country as his passport is invalid.

Gardaí have received a number of calls from people believing they have seen Mr Baxter but there have been no positive leads as yet.

Although he wears glasses, it is possible that he is not wearing them constantly as he does not rely on them on a permanent basis.

"He could also have rough stubble or a beard by now," said Kieran.

When last seen he was wearing a grey coat, black tracksuit and runners. Roman is described as 5' 11" with black/brown hair and blue eyes.

Anyone with information is asked to contact the gardaí in Bishopstown at (021) 4541012.

Husband of dead woman detained

AN IRISHMAN was still being questioned in Spain this morning after his wife's body was found in a holiday villa yesterday morning.

The body was found by police in Alicante after they were called to the house yesterday morning.

Police in Alicante detained the man at the scene.

Three children, believed to be aged one, three and eight, were also in the house at the time. They were being cared for by relatives.

The Department of Foreign Affairs would not give details today on where in Ireland the family is from.

"Our consular offices in Madrid are in regular touch with the Spanish authorities about this matter," said a spokeswoman.

---

from the Gulf.
"This is the big one," said Peter Beudel, an oil analyst with Cameron Hanover.

the Best Restaurant in Munster Award.

Joy for charities

● **From Page 1**.
Promotions and the O'Connor family,

Val O'Connor is well known for his charity work in the past, having been involved with Opera 2005, and the campaign to help refurbish Cork's North Cathedral. His generosity was recognised by the late Pope John Paul II, who in 2000 awarded Mr O'Connor a papal knighthood.

Mr Val and Finbarr O'Connor did not rule out the possibility of Cork playing host to another headline grabbing act in the future.

"The Bocelli concert has proved that Cork is capable of hosting such a magnificent event," said Finbarr. "In terms of a suitable venue, we have unearthed a gem in Collins Barracks," he added.

Deaths: Page 70

Evening Echo newspaper appeal

Evening Echo newspaper front page appeal

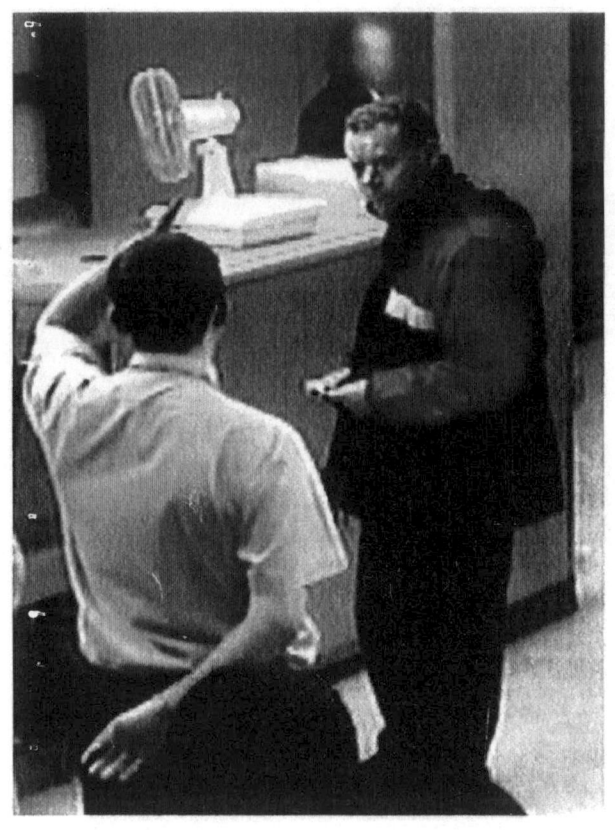

CCTV image of Ronan at Cork Airport

Part Two

September 3rd

The short flight was on schedule as we made our descent through the dazzling cloudscape and across the vast urban sprawl of West London. Blue skies. That particular low-sun blaze of September sunshine. Lower and lower, the dark silhouette of the plane shadowing us on the ground. The crunching squeal of tarmac and the roaring rush of the reverse thrust giving way to a frustratingly sedate spin to the terminal. Engine off. Lights on. The usual passenger pandemonium.

"Ladies and gentleman. Welcome to London Heathrow. The local time is one-thirty...

On time. Okay. Good.

"....exercise caution when opening the overhead lockers..."

Open the doors.

"...please remember to take all your belongings...."

Yeah, yeah. Just open the doors.

"...and on behalf of the captain and myself..."

Jesus Christ!

"…pleasant stay in the London area…"

Just open the doors.

"…thank you for choosing to travel with Aer Lingus…"

OPEN the doors!

"…Slán agus Beannacht."

JUST OPEN THE DOORS SO WE CAN OFF THIS PLANE AND FIND OUR BROTHER!!

Outside. Finally standing on the top step in the warm glare of the London sunshine, the apron shimmering before me in the heat, I paused to catch my breath – and gulped down the fetid mixture of aviation fumes and scorched air. Why had I been in such a mad rush to get off the plane? Where exactly was I going? I glanced over my shoulder at Martin. If I looked anything like him, we were a sorry sight. Stressed out and psyched up. Like two punch-drunk prize-fighters gearing up for the ring. Our eyes met and we shook our heads wordlessly.

"Sorry, sir, are you okay? Em, you're holding up the line...?"

Mumbling apologies, I made my way down the metal steps. The reality, the *enormity*, of the task before me settled on my shoulders like a physical weight. The truth was we were three weeks behind Ronan's arrival in London. He had once lived here for a time but I didn't know this place at all. This was not my home. In reality, Martin and myself were just two strangers in a foreign land, looking for a third. One that may not want to be found. One that may not be *findable*. One that could already be lost...

What can I actually do?

Stay calm and work systematically.

Where will I start?

At the beginning.

I'm completely out of my depth.

It'll be ok. You've come this far. Martin is here too. Two heads are better than one.

But it's impossible!

And yet, it has to be done.

It dawned on me that all the other passengers, and even some of the crew, had overtaken me; the ridiculous man who had nearly clamoured over people's shoulders to get off the plane only to take root at the door of the building. Martin had gone in.

And once I went through those doors, this would all become real again. I would have to be organised and sensible. Practical. Persuasive. I would have to resume a search which could end in pain and sorrow. Or nothing at all. Dad's parting words ripped at my heart.

A baggage truck trundled past, the driver in his hi-viz and noise-defenders.

"You aw'right, mate?"

Not really. My brother is missing and I have to find him.

"Yeah. Sorry. Must've just spaced out there for a minute."

"Well, you need to go on in, mate. It's a bit dodgy out here."

"Yeah, you're right, there. Yeah. Sorry."

So at last, feeling like a complete eejit, and with this futile nagging away inside my head, I hefted up my bag and strode into the noisy generic chaos of the Heathrow concourse.

A man of confidence and purpose.

A man on a mission.

Oh, fuck!

Martin's slumped shoulders eased back the minute he saw me. No rebuke for my inexplicable delay. The hint of a smile. C'mon. We were the Baxter boys. Together we would do everything we possibly could to find Ronan. All we needed was a bit of luck. Another little miracle or two. And he had already got the lay of the land. Bought us a couple of sandwiches and drinks, and even organised Tube tickets for our journey into the city centre. Jesus! How long had I been out there on the tarmac?

As we followed the throng to the Underground, I accepted this negativity was getting me nowhere. I needed to shake it off and get stuck into the job in hand

Once seated, I felt the frenetic energy of the London rush all around. The extraordinary array of passengers pressed together, squeezing on and off, and the occasional and inexplicable swoosh of hot wind. Martin didn't say a word, just kept an anxious eye on the overhead map so as not to miss our stop. But I found the rattle and sway of the Tube ride oddly soothing. It lulled my agitation, calmed my heartbeat. Drowned out the inner voices of doubt and fear. Once the train actually went underground, I found myself confronted by my own dark reflection. I looked tired and lined, a ghostly facsimile of my father. But I was real and solid. And I was here. Instinctively I conjured my mother's beautiful face in the dark grubby pane before me.

Please help us, Mum.

If only for Dad's sake, please help us now.

I'd only been to London once, and that was just a touristy weekend break many years before. I'd forgotten the sheer size and scale of the city. The Tube was noisy and crowded as we made our way to South Kensington station. Crammed with gesturing people of every nationality, colour, the babble of clashing languages and the jaded, long-suffering silence of the locals. As a result of our Irish media appeal, Jury's Kensington had kindly offered my brother-in-law, Gerry, discount-rate family accommodation for as long as necessary. This was one of those amazing and unexpected acts of kindness that kept us all going. Staying in central London was obviously ideal, but any protracted stay would have put terrible additional strain on the family without this assistance.

We came up and out of the Underground into the glare and warmth of the September sunshine. Kensington High Street. High-end boutiques and jewellers jostled with Indian takeaways and phone repair shops; well-appointed redbricks with bedsits. I thought how Mum would have relished a mooch around Harrods, mingling with the rich and famous. The palace gates where Princess Diana's flowers had overflowed onto the street would be around here somewhere.

But the brief walk from the Tube to the hotel was almost too much for me. I dragged my suitcase behind me with one hand and tried not to drop my laptop and underarm briefcase. I felt hot and cranky, happy for Martin to lead the way. Struggled to keep up. Every step I took in my new black shoes shot daggers of pain up through my back and into my neck. I recognised the signs. Just stress and anxiety taking its toll on me. After three weeks with little or no sleep, my body was crying out for rest.

As I limped my way along the pavement, I felt rather than saw the endless waves of people rushing by. With eyes fixed firmly on Martin's determined figure, I winced along on auto-pilot. Abruptly, my tired eyes honed in on a tall lean man walking a little ahead of me. At first, I couldn't understand why he'd caught my attention. There was nothing particularly striking about him. He was well-groomed and 'respectable', as Mum would have said, dressed in a black suit and white open-necked shirt. Then I got it. He was ambling. Taking his time. That was it. Moving in a slow aimless gait completely at odds with the rush; he was literally out of step with everyone around him. For some reason, I found this disturbing. Something wasn't right.

Just as I registered this thought, I lost sight of him when he suddenly dropped to his left. Oh my God! Was he ill? Is that why he was walking so slowly? I hurried to help. The poor man... But in the few seconds it took for the crowd in front of me to part and continue on their way unperturbed, I made sense of what was really going on. The shock! By now I was almost directly behind him. He didn't require help. He wasn't ill. He wasn't old. He was homeless. And hungry. He had simply spotted a half-eaten sandwich in an open street bin and pounced on it.

I looked on in horror as he resumed his slow peaceable walk ahead of me and wolfed down someone else's garbage. Here. In affluent, cosmopolitan London.

In the Royal Borough of Chelsea and Kensington, for God's sake.

This could be Ronan's fate if I don't find him.

Forgetting my tight new shoes and aching neck, I felt a stab of shame.

Okay, Mum. Thanks. I get it.

No more whinging. No more self-pity. This isn't about me. It's about Ronan.

Chastened now, and picking up my pace, I steered around the anonymous stroller, who maintained his own calm unhurried course to nowhere in particular, and made my way into Jury's luxurious lobby.

The receptionist welcomed us with a friendly handshake and an Irish accent. She somehow knew why we were in London, and efficiently checked us in, offered us the full facilities of the hotel and wished us success.

Room 302. Our temporary home. Who knew how long we'd be there for?

We quickly unpacked and organised the wi-fi. It was clear my laptop and carry-case would be the essential tools of our search going forward.

I had spoken to Dermot Keating by phone late on Friday evening. He had suggested we call to a number of key police stations in the London area over the weekend. He also told us there had been a number of 'sightings' of Ronan in London in the days immediately following August 13th. He would fill us in when we met us on the following Monday.

By late that afternoon, my carry-case was packed with pages and pages of essential contact phone numbers and email addresses and with numerous copies of the letter we had obtained from Ronan's medical consultant at home. We had also obtained a very clear image of Ronan from the Cork Airport CCTV footage which Maria and Joey had managed to get enlarged and laminated for another Missing Person poster before we'd left. The new poster included details of the UK contact number provided by Dermot Keating and showed Ronan wearing his red and blue jacket and navy tracksuit trousers as he checked in for his flight to London.

Dermot had listed the ten key police stations in the London area and recommended that we personally visit each of them. We decided to work inwards from Heathrow Airport to the centre of London. Armed with our documents and posters and a map of the Tube system, Martin and I headed for the South Kensington Tube station. It was early evening and the sun was still shining brightly as we entered the station. But before buying a ticket, I impulsively decided to seek the help of the security attendant standing at the turnstile. He was small and stocky, with the full head of grey hair and white beard of an Anglo-Indian. With a warm smile he quickly explained the various daily and weekly ticket options.

I pulled out a copy of our Missing Person poster and asked if we could display it on the nearby notice-board. His expression immediately grew serious as he guided us to the side of the notice-board and introduced himself as Tanaka. He asked about all about Ronan; how long he'd been missing; where we were staying.

As we pinned our poster to the board, Tanaka explained how he himself had come to London from India as a young boy with his parents. He'd married his childhood sweetheart and they had three sons, all of whom were also now living and working in London. He shook both our hands as we went on our way, and bade us to keep faith, promising he would pray for Ronan's safe return.

And so a new friend was made. Each day, every morning and evening from then on, Tanaka would hurry to greet us at South Kensington

Station to ask about our progress. And every day he urged us to keep our spirits up, to keep the faith in our search.

I must admit, that first evening I felt just a little bit more secure in the vast concrete jungle that we were about to navigate. The support of family and friends is a wonderful thing.

But the kindness of strangers never ceases to amaze me.

We decided to start with Hounslow and Twickenham Police. At each station we asked to see the Sergeant in Charge, posted our Missing Persons poster on the main notice-board, handed in a copy of the consultant's letter, waited to ensure Ronan's details and our new Jury's address and contact phone numbers were logged on the system, and promised to return within a few days. We finished the evening with visits to the stations at Bishopsgate, Wood Street and Snow Hill. By the time Martin and I had returned to Jury's, the bright evening sunshine had given way to a dark, warm haze which settled over the city lights.

We got no further than the foyer before collapsing into two armchairs. We were exhausted.

But time was running out. Ronan's lack of medication was becoming a critical issue. There was more work to be done. I prepared an updated UK Press Release which summarised our family's appeal for help, stated that Martin and I were now in London, and included our new address and contact numbers. It rounded off with an appeal for any assistance in the search to find Ronan. We worked through most of the night sending the new Press Release to every London media and humanitarian organisation email contact. The only interruptions to our work came from the occasional expression of concern by the hotel concierge or the odd tipsy hotel guest returning after a night on the town.

September 4th

Sunday morning broke before we knew it. Breakfast was early and pretty much on the run as we reviewed any email copies received overnight and confirmed that all the emails we'd sent the previous day had found their target addresses. Martin called home with updates, while I worked away on the laptop. On the surface, Dad was holding up well at home, and proclaiming a new sense of hope. Inside I knew he was suffering with the same crippling uncertainty every one of us was struggling with.

Preparation done, we headed off to the Heathrow Airport police. We had decided to start with the police station and then use the afternoon to pin our posters around the various terminals. Passing through South Kensington Tube on our way, I was once again strengthened by the concern and good wishes of Tanaka. My optimism level was high.

While we made our now well-rehearsed presentation to the Sergeant in Charge at

Heathrow Airport Police station, I sensed an increased sense of security and hesitancy. The Sergeant informed us that there had been a number of 'sightings' of Ronan around Terminals 4 and 5 on August 15th and 16th. This meant Ronan was already logged on the airport police system. He explained that 'sightings' refer to interventions by the airport police when a person is stopped and checked, in cases of loitering or acting suspiciously in airport terminals or surrounding areas. For security purposes a Form 5090 known as a 'Stop and Search Notice', is completed and issued for each intervention, and a copy logged on the airport police computer system.

I drew a number of deep breaths as the sergeant spoke, and felt an empty, gut-wrenching pain in my stomach. We now knew that Ronan had definitely spent at least two days in Heathrow Airport. He had somehow managed to enter the country on a Bus Pass, but there was absolutely no chance he would be allowed fly home again from Heathrow or indeed from any UK airport.

If he was still alive, he was alone.

Without medication, and most likely, without money.

Somewhere in London.

We thanked the Sergeant in Charge for this troubling update and left, heading back through the terminals in a blur of numb hopelessness. We spent the rest of Sunday afternoon wandering around each terminal. Searching. Hoping against hope, Ronan would still be there.

But we were three weeks too late.

We knew that even as we searched on in silence.

The Tube ride back to South Kensington was silent and sombre. There was nothing to say. Even Tanaka's kindness couldn't lift our spirits. The sweet old man gave us every word of encouragement he could think of, but Martin and I were beyond comfort, spiralling into despair. It was agonising. If only we'd known sooner that Ronan had flown to London. If we had found out immediately after the August 13th, there would have been a very real chance that we would have found Ronan at Heathrow Airport. He'd be at home now in Cork, instead of lost and alone in London.

It was late evening as we approached the door to Jurys. Outside, sitting on the pavement about twenty yards short of the door, sat a solitary man. As we passed, he held out his hand for money. We stopped. I asked him his name. 'Vincent'. We chatted for some time as Vincent explained that he had come from Paris earlier in the summer hoping to get a job in London, but nothing had materialised. He had run out of cash and he was now homeless. I showed Vincent our Missing Person poster. I knew it was a long-shot. He shook his head. He hadn't seen Ronan.

It came to me that I'd never had a conversation with a homeless person before. I don't know what I was expecting, but just like my solitary walker, Vincent opened my eyes. He was, well …he was a *person*. Vincent looked about thirty-five to forty years of age. He spoke good English with an attractive French lilt. When I asked him where he slept at night, he stood and gestured for us to follow him.

In the centre of the busy road, almost directly opposite Jury's Hotel, the traffic zoomed round a large flowered island. The flower beds were surrounded by a low two-foot wall and finished with a large cap stone which tilted inwards towards the centre. From the safe distance of the pavements running either side, it acted as a pretty but fairly innocuous division for the two lanes of traffic. But following Vincent when he stepped over the surrounding wall inside the flower beds, we could see that he had scooped out the earth to provide a nest where he could bed down under the cover of the cap stone and be all but invisible to the passing world. A rucksack and sleeping bag lay rolled against the inside of the wall on the bare soil.

The noise and fumes from the traffic were intense, yet Vincent's basic shelter was only a stone's throw away from our plush hotel at the other side of the road.

The day that was in it; the irony of the situation; it was all too much for us.

Too much harsh reality.

Martin pressed a twenty pound note into Vincent's hand and his open Gallic face lit up in a broad smile. We left Vincent to his urban burrow and entered the hotel. In its own way, this encounter had done me some good. I realised the homeless man was just a regular guy, down on his luck. Things just got away from him.

There but for the grace of God…

My brother was somewhere out there in London tonight. I hoped and prayed he was safe, fed, sheltered.

Because even in the comfort of this beautiful hotel, I felt battered and defected.

And we still had to give Dad the body-blow of what we'd found at Heathrow earlier in the day.

How would he take it?

It was the lowest I'd felt since our search had begun.

September 5th

We'd put together a pretty hectic schedule for Monday. We had to make the most of every minute in London. Precious time was slipping through our fingers. And on top of the full itinerary Martin and I had planned, I'd lain awake half the night, hatching a plan. It was a long-shot, but with a bit of luck, and bare-faced cheek, it might just work...

Meantime, we'd arranged to meet Dermot Keating in Scotland Yard at half nine. He stressed the need to come in good time as it would take at least thirty minutes to pass through security clearance. We also brought passports for identification purposes. Despite the heat, Martin and I dressed in smart jackets and trousers. First impressions count, and I felt it was important to look smart today. Looking like two professional businessmen would also help my plan along...

Our taxi driver on our eight o'clock ride to Scotland Yard was a typical cockney. Friendly and chatty. I couldn't help being reminded of Barry

Evans in The Adventures of a Taxi Driver. This cheery thought temporarily lightened the load as we headed into another stressful day of searching. As he negotiated his way through the madness of the rush-hour traffic, he asked what we were doing in London; business or pleasure? I told him we were in London to find Ronan, my brother. 'Whereabouts is he, guvs?' he asked. As I explained that he was missing and we were here to find him, his chirpy demeanour instantly evaporated. With a look of utter disbelief on his face, he spent the rest of our journey basically warning us not to get our hopes up. London was a vast city. People like Ronan went missing every day. They are seldom, if ever, found.

I felt a brief surge of indignation. What an insensitive eejit! How could he crush our hopes this way? Be so oblivious to what we were going through? Then Martin caught my eye. Put his hand on my arm. No point wasting emotional energy on this. The guy didn't mean any harm. We were just a couple of punters in the back of his cab. Strangers. He didn't know us, or how far we'd go to find our brother. How could he?

With a deep breath, I sat back and gathered myself while the taxi-driver rumbled on.

I tuned out. Didn't listen.

Today I had a new focus and determination.

As Dermot had predicted, it took the bones of an hour to get through security at the entrance to Scotland Yard. The process was boring and officious but only reinforced how lucky we were to have such high-ranking connections in the UK police. There's no way we would have made it inside this bastion of British law-enforcement otherwise. Having finally satisfied themselves that we were who we said we were, we were given name tags to be worn at all times in the building.

Dermot appeared in the foyer with his ever-steady handshake and reassuring smile and we followed him to the nearby lifts and headed for the upper floors. We chatted away, filling him in on our efforts and progress as we followed him through busy labyrinthine offices. Phones ringing. Uniformed and plain-clothes personnel dashing around. Frenetic activity. People getting on with the job. No messing about. Good. And then we stopped outside a grey double door.

The Missing Persons Department.

Another belt to the gut. The taxi driver was right. So many people went missing, they had a huge department dedicated to finding them. And mostly, they didn't.

Oh, God…

My stupid shoes were still killing me, and I focused on putting one sore foot in front of another to distract me from these useless thoughts. We stepped through the door where we were amazed to be introduced to Ravi Pillai, Deputy Head of New Scotland Yard. He took a pleasant but pragmatic approach, and we listened intently as he told us of the thousands of missing persons listed in the London Missing Persons computer system. In fact, the department did not actively look for those missing persons at all. Actually, there was no direct link between the database of the Missing Persons Unit and all the individual police stations in the London area. The Scotland Yard unit simply deleted the names from the list when those persons were reported found, whether dead or alive. This explained why Dermot had told us to visit all the key London police stations.

Dermot then informed us that Ronan had been 'stopped' by airport police in Heathrow Airport on three separate occasions: in Terminal 4 at 3pm on August at 15th, and again in Terminal 4 at 5pm on the same day. Finally, he had been removed from Terminal 3 after being stopped again the following day of August 16th. Dermot went on to explain that Ronan had been driven out of the airport by the airport police and 'ejected' at Hatton Cross.

Although we'd already been given a broad outline of these facts the previous day, the news that Ronan had been ejected from the airport had not been mentioned. We were now more shocked than surprised at this revelation. We were already beginning to harden to the hidden and harsh underbelly of this huge impersonal city. On the other hand, both Ravi and Dermot had been kind enough to give us their expertise, vital insights into the police system and invaluable advice which might help us find Ronan.

There was nothing else to do but sincerely thank them for their time and efforts, while Dermot promised to keep us in the loop with any developments as they arose.

Before coming to London, almost everyone told us it would virtually impossible to break into the London media. Yet it was obvious that the London media would be the key to finding Ronan.

And despite the general lack of optimism, we somehow managed to get our first breakthrough.

I had arranged a meeting with Amanda Diamond, a reporter with the *Irish Post* newspaper, outside Scotland Yard that Monday at twelve noon. She had received my Press Releases and emailed me to confirm she would be running a story on Ronan in that week's edition of the newspaper. She was also bringing a press photographer to get a photograph of Martin and myself standing in front of the iconic Scotland Yard sign that morning. As the *Irish Post* has the highest circulation figures amongst the London Irish community, this proved to be a major first step in harnessing the London media in our search to find Ronan.

Sometimes desperate times call for desperate measures. As we waited for the reporter and photographer outside the imposing tower of

New Scotland Yard, I reved up my courage, put on my game face, and dialled the Irish Embassy in London. With as much casual authority as I could muster, I gave my name and asked to be put through to Mr. Ray Walker, the Embassy Press Attaché. The receptionist politely told me that Mr. Walker was out on business but would briefly be in his office between 2pm and 3pm. I declined to leave a message with the pleasant and efficient receptionist and brazenly lied that I would ring Ray on his mobile instead.

Martin stared at me in disbelief. My plan was in motion. But before I could fill Martin in, Amanda Diamond and her photographer, Malcolm McNally, turned up. Everything went fine and we were delighted to hear that the weekly edition would hit the shelves the following day and carry a major news article on Ronan. This was real progress. We were on a roll.

We arrived at the front entrance to the Irish Embassy in Grosvenor Place, Belgravia around a quarter to two. To say the whole area was imposing is putting it mildly. Shades of a forgotten Empire. Pretty much on the doorstep of Buckingham Palace and Westminster. Elegant listed Georgian and Victorian mansions flew the flags of their home nations. Brass plaques. Visible security presence…

I had warned Martin to stick close and say nothing. Clasping my briefcase firmly, I took a deep breath and strode towards the porticoed entryway purposely. *Ambasáid na hÉireann.*

Here goes nothing…

We were stopped by a security man. I smiled, flashed my Irish passport, and explained we had a meeting with Mr. Ray Walker at two o'clock. Proceed. At the front door we were stopped by a police officer. Once again I showed my passport and said we were here for a two o'clock meeting with Mr. Walker. The large front door swung open and we approached an attractive blonde woman sitting behind a big mahogany desk. In front of her, a small, discreet sign bore the single word 'Reception'.

I introduced myself and reminded her that I had phoned earlier that morning. Of course she had remembered my call. I went on to say that

I had caught up with Ray on his mobile and he had agreed to meet me at the Embassy at 2pm. Eventhough I fully expected her to press some kind of alarm button and have us removed, I kept a confident smile plastered on my face.

And somehow, unbelievably, my scam worked. We were directed to wait in his office as he would be along shortly.

It was only once we were actually through the door and left to our devices, that I felt a bit panicky.

Jesus! What the hell have I just done?

This wasn't just pushing the boundaries - it was probably some kind of offence. Would we too be 'ejected'? From the Embassy? From the UK? No. We were Irish citizens, on Irish territory. We were entitled to ask for the help of our government. Still…

As we more or less collapsed into the two large Victorian armchairs in front of Ray Walker's desk, I could feel Martin's eyes on me. He didn't say one word. Still stunned by my audacity. So we sat there in sickening silence until the door eventually burst open and a genial, slightly flustered man apologised for keeping us waiting. He hadn't realised we had arranged a meeting with him.

We stood and we introduced ourselves with extended handshakes. I immediately came clean – what else could I do? – and quickly explained that we needed to just five minutes of his time on a matter of life or death to my family.

Before he could protest, I pressed a copy of our latest Press Release, Ronan's medical consultant's letter, and the Missing Person poster into his hands. Ray sat down and carefully studied the documents. We waited with baited breath. When he reached forward and picked up the handset of the phone, I was sure this was the end of us.

Deep breath…

There was a genuine possibility that he was going to call security, or worse, the police.

Another deep breath…

The receptionist answered. And then the instruction from Ray to cancel all his appointments for that afternoon as something urgent and unexpected had come up.

A wave of pure relief swept over Martin and myself.

He was going to help us.

We spent the next two and a half hours with Ray. Once he had every detail of Ronan's case, he phoned every media contact and humanitarian organisation in the London area that he could think of. While he took down details, I made a note of the contact name in every case. As the Press Attaché to the Irish Embassy, he had media contacts all over London. With each phone call, Ray gave a brief summary of Ronan's case and explained that both Martin and I were now in London searching for our missing brother. He also stressed the medical urgency of finding Ronan as soon as possible. Once again, we stunned at the humanity of strangers.

It was close to five when we finally left Ray with our heartfelt thanks. He gave me his email address and direct phone number and I promised to keep him updated. He wished us well in our search for Ronan and hoped that we would find him alive and safe. As we walked out of the Irish Embassy, I felt ten stone lighter and a renewed sense of optimism

The evening was warm and balmy. It had been a busy and eventful day. We decided to head to nearby Hyde Park. I needed to catch up on my phone messages and we both needed some respite from the day. We found a park bench close to Speakers' Corner. We sat in the calming sunshine and discussed the day's events. As I listened to my many messages, Martin approached two passing police officers. He showed them Ronan's Missing Person's poster. The police officers did not recognise Ronan. The officers pointed in the direction of an area of the park where the homeless tended to gather. They explained that it was about a five or ten minute walk and could be worth checking.

We gathered our thoughts and headed in the direction the police officers had pointed to. We talked as we walked.

As we approached an area by a small lake, the sound of raucous talking and shouting made me feel a little nervous. Growing closer, we made out a large group of maybe ten or fifteen people, mostly men, sitting on the grass at the side of the lake. It was an isolated area and there was no one else to be seen. They all looked rough and dirty and nearly all were drinking from cans or bottles. There was a lot of banter and shouting loudly at each other. I let Martin walk forward as I drew up the rear.

The minute the group saw us, they started to gesture loudly and I felt sure we were going to be robbed and mugged at the very least. But Martin kept his cool and approached the group peaceably. He waved the poster of Ronan and shouted a plea for help. Once things settled a little, he managed to explain that we were looking for Ronan who was from Ireland.

Within the space of thirty seconds, silence descended on the group and then someone shouted the suggestion to check a local soup kitchen address. And then another and another. I noted the details of each suggestion. I could just about make out an Irish accent from the majority as they spoke.

While none had seen Ronan, an air of genuine concern and comradery had fallen over the group. I didn't know what to make of this. I was somewhere between astounded and saddened.

We had stumbled upon a group of homeless people in the middle of Hyde Park and most of them sounded Irish. They had almost nothing in this world, yet they wanted to help a fellow Irish person who was missing in London.

Perhaps deep down each of them secretly hoped that someone would come looking for them and rescue them someday. I wondered exactly how these poor souls had ended up homeless in London. I wondered how long many would survive. My hope was that someday soon someone would rescue them. But I thought of Vincent. The problem was at a far greater scale than I'd ever imagined.

And as we returned to our hotel later that night, there sat our new French friend in the exact same spot as he'd been the night before. He'd obviously chosen this 'patch' as a good place to beg. And his logic was clear. It was close enough to Jury's to do well from the relatively affluent passers-by and visitors to the hotel. Although I felt guilty about it, I was just too worn down and my heart was broken after our encounter in the park, to spend much time with him. Instead we gave him all our loose change and headed into the sanctuary of the hotel.

It had been a full and busy day and I was aching with physical and emotional fatigue. But I had still one last job to do before I could sleep. I had to resend my Press Release to the London newspapers as a follow-up to the phone calls Ray Walker had made from the Irish Embassy.

The last email I sent that night was to Ray Walker, to thank him from the bottom of our hearts for his support and unstinting assistance earlier in the day.

September 6ᵗʰ

The following morning we came down for breakfast at nine. Another busy day loomed ahead as we had decided to visit as many of the remaining police stations in the London area as possible. To do this, we spent a while mapping out a list of the police stations and travel by Tube. As I finished breakfast, I reviewed my emails. Martin, in good spirits, joked that he did not want any more near arrest experiences or surprises. I kidded that I did not want any more near muggings.

My phone rang. I recognised the number immediately. Dermot Keating. He was excited and focused. Ronan had been located in Hounslow. He was being held by police officers outside the park entrance at North Street, Isleworth. However our brother couldn't be arrested or detained indefinitely as he had done nothing wrong. Dermot urged us to get the Tube to Hounslow and a taxi from the Tube station to North Street.

Oh, my God. Oh, my God. We've got to hurry…

Trying to keep my emotions in check, I rose from the breakfast table a little unsteadily. It seemed too good to be true.

Deep breath…

My phone rang again. As it was a UK phone number, I decided to answer the call. It was the London Times newspaper. The editor explained that the paper had decided to run an article on Ronan's case later in the week. He wanted to arrange a meeting with me. I thanked him, took his phone number and promised to phone him back. It was ironic that we had broken into the London media just as Ronan had been located.

We sat in tense silence on the never-ending Tube ride to Hounslow. It was hard to know how to feel. Would we be too late again? How would Ronan be? Would he actually want to come home with us? Outside the station we quickly found a taxi to take us to the park entrance on North Street. Martin and I said very little. I was engulfed by wave after wave of emotion.

Please, Mum. Let him be there. Let him be safe….

It was like each wave of emotion was wrapping me in warm cotton wool. It was an eerie sensation.

Deep breath...

My mind raced.

As we approached the park entrance, I made out the police car. Two police officers were standing on the pavement chatting to someone dressed in a red and blue jacket.

It was our Ronan.

Our driver pulled up, oblivious to the human drama unfolding around him. We hurled ourselves out of the taxi and ran to our brother. He recognised us immediately and broke down in a torrent of sobs. Tears poured down his face. We weren't far behind him. Martin and myself each put our arms around him, drawing him into us, cradling him in a Baxter huddle. The elation of the moment was indescribable. At that moment nothing else mattered in the world. We were completely euphoric.

Ronan was coming home with us and would get all the love and care he needed. Dad was going to see his son again. As we stood there in the middle of the busy London street - laughing and crying and hugging and explaining all at once – my thoughts strayed to Vincent and the homeless people in the park. To what Ronan's fate might have been.

Thanks, Mum. Never stop looking after us…

Because she *must* have been looking over us.

Finding Ronan in London was little short of a miracle

The police explained that a local North Street resident had gone to the local shop that morning. She picked up the early edition of the Irish Post newspaper which carried a full front-page article on Ronan with FIND RONAN in bold type.

As she walked home from the shop, she noticed that someone wearing a red and navy jacket was trying to set fire to rubbish at the park entrance. It looked to be the same person as the photograph in the paper. She could have left it. Not got involved. But thank God she didn't do that. Instead she phoned Hounslow Police Station. The officer in charge checked the name on the police station computer database. Since we had called to the same station a few days earlier, Ronan's full case history and contact phone numbers now appeared on the system. The officer in charge requested a car. Two police officers from the neighbouring Chiswick police station offered to take the call.

And, hey presto, Ronan was found.

Officer Brett Page and his colleague were both originally from Scotland. They immediately understood the significance and improbability of what had just happened. Something wonderful and almost impossible had been achieved. They offered to call an ambulance or to take us to a hospital in the police car. We asked Ronan if he would go to the hospital with us so that he could be checked over. He avoided direct eye contact with us and stared down. Though he said very little, he agreed. He looked disorientated and dishevelled. He wore the same red and navy jacket and navy tracksuit trousers that he had worn more than three weeks earlier in Cork Airport.

While we waited for the ambulance to arrive, I grabbed the chance to call Sally. It was a school day, and I was surprised when my daughter answered the phone.

"Hello?"

"Hi, Lisa. No school? Are you sick, love…?"

"Hi Dad. Ah, no. Just have a little sore throat - but Mum said I could stay home today. But *you* sound a bit weird, Dad. Are *you* okay?"

"No, I'm grand. I'm *great*. I'm here with Ronan. We found him! Where's Mum?"

"Oh, my God! Dad! That's…oh, my God, that's fantastic! Hold on. I think she's out in the garden. Mum? MUUUUUUM!! Dad's on the phone….*MUM*! They found Ronan…"

The phone clanked. I heard the tinny faraway sounds of doors banging, muffled words, footsteps running….Then Sally.

"Ciaran? You really found him? Where was he? What did he say…? Is he…is he all right?"

"Hi Sals. Yeah…I mean, I think so. We're not sure. I don't know yet. It's all a bit …emotional you know. Overwhelming. I'm just giving you a quick buzz while the police sort out the hospital…"

"Hospital? The *police*…?"

"No, no, it's fine. The police are really nice - just helping us. I can't really talk now, Sal – we're under pressure here to get things sorted out. I'll explain everything later. We're somewhere in Hounslow. I just couldn't wait to tell you. We *found* him, Sally! I can't believe it..."

There was a pause. I could hear my girls snuffling...

"Hello? Are ye okay? Are ye crying?

"Yeah. No. I mean, a bit, yeah. I don't know whether to laugh or cry...it's so... I mean, I began to think..."

"Yeah."

"...in my heart of hearts, I wasn't sure ye could do it..."

"I know."

"*Jesus*, Ciaran. It's incredible. It's...its *wonderful!*"

"It is. It really is..."

"He's alive. But have you got hold of your Dad yet? The poor man is beside himself..."

"Yeah, of course, of course. Martin is going to ring him this minute."

"Okay so. But, listen…I still…I just can't take it in. Where are you now? How has he been….?"

"Somewhere in Hounslow. It's all a bit… Look, I have to go, love. I'll call you tonight, okay…"

"Wait, wait! Ciaran?"

"Yeah?"

"I don't know. Just…I mean, wow. Take a breath. You did it. You actually found Ronan."

"We all did it."

The police officers took us to West Middlesex Hospital in Isleworth. While the officers explained Ronan's situation to the nurse in the A&E, Martin and I sat with Ronan in the large waiting room.

As we waited, I checked what my brother had with him. From somewhere deep inside the blue and red jacket, he produced his battered Irish bus pass, AIB Bank Deposit Book, and an old prescription for his medication. In his tracksuit pants pocket, he jangled two pounds coins and the front door key to our house. He also pulled out the crumpled 'Stop and Search' Notice issued by Heathrow Airport Police in Terminal 4 on

August 15th. These few bits and pieces and the clothes he stood up in were all he had to his name.

When I considered how much longer he could have survived in London in this condition, my heart went across me. We had somehow managed to rescue him from the cliff-edge; from the abyss.

Deep breath…

Ronan was admitted to West Middlesex University Hospital later that afternoon. We profusely thanked the two police officers who had brought us to the hospital, and offered them hospitality and accommodation if they were ever in Cork. Martin and I liaised with the doctors and completed all the necessary paperwork. We also provided all the contact details and phone numbers for Ronan's medical consultant in Ireland. They confirmed that Ronan was actually extremely ill and would to need to stay in hospital for a number of weeks. But he was now safe and in good hands.

The day had been completely absorbed with the formalities of the situation, and every time we had picked up the phone to call Dad something else had demanded our attention. After Ronan's admission, I grabbed a quick breath of air in the autumn sunshine of the hospital entrance while Martin finally called Dad with the news. On the speaker, my father's strained and resigned voice was almost inaudible against the to and fro of the bustling hospital doorway.

"Well, Martin? Any news?"

"Yes, the best news, Dad. We found Ronan! He's fine… Dad? *Dad*?"

Complete silence.

"Dad? *Dad*! Are you okay?"

"No, no, I'm here. I'm here. I…I can't believe it. And, you're sure it's him?"

"It is, Dad. It's Ronan. We're here with him right now at the hospital…"

"Hospital? Oh, no! What hospital? Is he very sick? What condition is he in?"

"Yeah, we're in West Middlesex. He's just been admitted. He's okay but he needs care. But he's in good hands now. Safe and sound."

"Really? You're sure he's okay, Martin?"

"He's fine, Dad. A bit disorientated and tired. But he knew us and he was delighted to see us. He'll be right as rain after some proper food and rest."

"Oh, thank God. Thank God. My prayers are answered…"

"I know. Myself and Ciaran feel the same, Dad. We can't take it in…"

"But how…?"

"A woman found him."

"A woman? What woman?"

"We don't know, Dad. A woman. She recognised him from the picture in the local paper…"

"Oh, right…"

"Yeah. She made the connection between the picture and a man she'd seen near the park. So she rang the police and…"

"Oh, the good woman, the good woman. Thank God, thank God…"

"…and they found him, and held on to him 'til we got there. It was earlier today, Dad, but it's been so hectic sorting everything out that I couldn't…"

"Yes, yes, but he's alright, Martin? You're not holding anything back now? Not keeping anything from me? You have to tell me everything."

"He's fine, Dad. Really. Ciaran is standing here beside me. He'll tell you the same…"

"No, no. I'm just…I'd nearly given up. I was demented…I…"

"I know, Dad, I know. But honest to God, he's alive and safe in his hospital bed."

"Oh, Martin. Thanks be to God and his Blessed Mother. My prayers are answered."

"But listen, Dad, please don't tell everyone yet, okay? It's really important that you don't. Just tell the girls and Aidan and Brian for now. Ciaran will sort things out with the Press in good time for the morning. But we want to settle Ronan into hospital before the news breaks. He needs a bit of rest and quiet…"

"Of course, of course. Whatever ye say. But when can he come home?"

"I'm not sure yet. He's still being assessed. But it might be a while. Why don't you ask the girls to sort out a flight for you to come here?"

"Yes. I'll do that so. Good idea. I won't believe he's okay 'til I see him with my own two eyes…"

"Trust me, Dad. He is okay. Ronan is safe now."

"Ah, God is good, Martin. The weight is after lifting off my heart. My prayers are answered."

"We need to go back into him now, Dad, okay? Be with him, you know?"

"Ye do of course. Go on so. And Martin?

"Yeah?"

"Tell him I'm on my way and I can't wait to see him."

"He'll be delighted, Dad."

"You should see my face, Martin. I'm after seeing myself in the hall mirror. I'm smiling like a cat that got the cream!"

He rang off.

After his initial disbelief, our father's joy and palpable relief that Ronan had been found was infectious. A wave of sheer happiness rolled over us again and we flung our arms around each other in a bear-hug. Our search was really over. The needle in the giant haystack had been found.

Next I called Dermot Keating in Scotland Yard, and Tony Quilter in Ireland, and thanked them from the bottom of my heart on behalf of myself and my family. I asked them not to disclose the fact that Ronan had been found until the following day as I needed time to get Ronan settled in hospital. We also needed time to prepare for the media circus which was about to follow. They were both completely understanding and agreed.

I had made a solemn promise to Barry in the Irish Press Association some weeks previously. I had given him my word that I would get back to him with an exclusive when I had found Ronan. It was now time to fulfil my promise, so I called him from the hospital that afternoon. He was stunned into silence by our success in finding Ronan. I committed to sending a full Press Release later that evening but asked him not to release it until 9am the following day. Once again, I stressed the fragility of Ronan's health and the time needed time to get him settled in hospital. He readily agreed and offered his good wishes for Ronan's speedy recovery. Once again, words were hardly enough, but I thanked Barry for his trust and help.

That evening Martin and myself made our way back to Jury's in Kensington. Once again we met Vincent in his usual place. Although he was delighted to hear we had found Ronan, I think it was bittersweet news. Our brother had been rescued, but his own bleak outlook looked to be unchanged. I felt so bad for him. It was a cruel and unforgiving world we lived in. We emptied our pockets and headed in. What else could we do?

Later that night, while Martin made all our family and close friend calls, I prepared a new Press Release stating that Ronan had been located in London, and was now safe and receiving appropriate medical care. I thanked the Gardaí, the London Metropolitan Police, the public, the media, and the various organisations for their incredible help and support. I finished by asking that the media respect our need for privacy to ensure Ronan's wellbeing and return to full health. I sent the new Press Release to Barry in the Irish Press Association at midnight that night. I knew that he would also send it on to the London Press Office. I sent another copy to Ray Walker of the Irish Embassy in London.

The job was finished.

Our search was over.

Happy and grateful, but tired to my bones, I dropped like a stone onto the bed, convinced I'd be asleep before my head hit the pillow.

But sleep didn't come.

The room was too hot and stuffy. I felt breathless and headachy. The events of the day, of the whole long search for Ronan, kept running through my mind like one endless and exhausting slide-show. Every time I felt my eyelids drooping and my mind sinking into blissful darkness, the heavy London traffic, a pulsing throb of car music, or the shrill and seemingly endless stream of emergency sirens jolted me from my rest again. After about an hour of churning about in the hot tangled sheets, I was getting beyond myself. I sat up, gulped down some water, and punched my pillows into shape.

It was something of a relief to hear Martin's calm voice in the darkness.

"You okay there, Ciaran? Can't get off to sleep?"

"Who are ya telling?"

"No. Me either."

"Yeah, sorry, sorry. I'm a bit cranky. Is it me, or this room very hot tonight?"

"I dunno. Feels the same to me…"

"Well, it doesn't to me. My head is banging and the street noise is unbelievable tonight …"

"Yeah…it's loud all right. D'you remember Mum used to say kids can't sleep when they're overtired?

"I do remember that. And it still doesn't make a shred of sense to me."

"I know. But that's what she used to say - and she did have seven of us, in fairness…"

"Yeah, well, I'm not overtired, Martin."

"Really? That's some impression you're doing there, then…"

"Oh, this is ridiculous! I mean, everything is fine, for God's sake! More than fine. Excellent. Perfect. I can't make it out. Ronan is safe. Back from the brink. It's nothing short of a miracle!

And *we'll* be back home with our families ourselves, asleep in our own beds this time tomorrow night. Life is good. Fantastic! Couldn't be better! So why do I feel so stressed out? God, my whole body is aching with weariness. So why can't I just switch off and get some sleep?"

"Do you really want to know?"

"Martin, I'm really not able for this right now…"

"Maybe because everything is *not* fine. Because life is *not* good."

"What? It is not…*what?* Jesus, what now? What are you saying…?"

"I'm not saying anything. Take it easy…"

"Don't tell me to take it easy! Look, it's two in the morning, and I'm lying here *sweating* in the dark, and after everything that's happened, I'm kinda losing it. What are you…?"

"Ciaran, listen. Relax. I'm not trying to annoy you. I'm only saying; yes, everything is fine *for us*. Life is good *for us*. It's so amazing that we found Ronan."

"It is!"

"I can't believe it. I'm totally pinching myself! We've been incredibly fortunate and the support and help we've had from friends and strangers has been a godsend."

"Exactly!"

"How we didn't get fired out of the Embassy on our arses I'll never know…"

"Yeah, we had the four-leafed shamrock there."

"And then that woman phoning the police when she saw Ronan."

"I know - fair play to her."

"And we may never know who, but someone somewhere must have helped Roman, fed him…"

"God, you're right…"

"So the Baxters are safe and I'm so grateful, so thankful, for this happy-ending."

"Yes, yes. Martin, of course. I am too. So what exactly is your point?"

"My point is not everyone gets a happy ending. So however hot it is or it isn't in this room tonight, I can't help but be aware that we are *in* a room, you know? Safe. Comfortable. Sheltered. I don't know about you, but I can't stop thinking about Vincent, not a hundred yards away from us here, bedding down in a dirty flower-bed in the middle of the road. 'Cos we know him now. And we can't un-know him. And we know he's just a regular man, just an ordinary person, who's down on his luck.

I can't even imagine how it must feel to live the way he does, can you? The reality of it, I mean. No shelter. Nowhere to cook a bite of food, to keep your belongings. No toilet or place to have a wash. No privacy of any kind. Utter exposure. Total vulnerability. My mind doesn't even know how to go there. And the fact that it's the twenty-first century in one of the richest cities in the world just makes it worse. How can this be? Jesus, Ciaran, we wouldn't leave our dogs at home in this condition!"

"Okay, but…"

"And we've met lots of other homeless people in the last few days. Destitutes, drunks, people eating out of dustbins, people struggling with mental health issues. People who haven't got the price of a ticket home, and don't know if they'd be welcomed back if they did. Now we don't just know *about* homelessness, about poverty - we've *seen* it first-hand."

"Yeah, yeah it's terrible…"

"So it wouldn't be normal, I don't think we could call ourselves human beings, if that didn't affect us. 'Cos we understand now how easy it is to slip down, to fall between the cracks, to become lost. And that's not the sort of thing you can ignore…"

"No…"

"So I don't know about you, but *that's* what coming between me and my sleep tonight. The conflicting emotions of it all, you know? I'm just as tired as you. And I'm just as happy and relieved as you. Everything you've been through, I've been through too. Every doubt and fear you've felt, I've felt too. Of course I'm nearly off my head with joy when I think of Ronan safe and well, reunited with us all, and back at home with Dad. But that doesn't stop me feeling devastated, guilty, ashamed even, when I think of Vincent and all the others…and I think its going stay with me for a long while."

"Yeah…"

"Of course, I may just be tired and homesick."

"We both are…"

"Ah, sweet Jesus, it's very late. Three o'clock, I don't even know what I'm saying, at this stage…"

"No, I think you do know, Martin, you do. And you're right. Thanks."

The quiet settled down on us as I finally surrendered to the lovely sleepy heaviness of my limbs and eyes.

"God, I can't wait to get back into my own bed with Sally tomorrow night."

"Whey-hey, Romeo. Bit of romance on the cards so?"

"You never know. But it's more that she doesn't snore like you all night long. Bloody hell! I thought I was bad!"

"Ah, Jesus! Just go to sleep, will ya!"

September 7th

There was a new sense of joy and tranquility over breakfast the following morning. The time ticked by as we waited for reactions to my Press Release which Barry had agreed to issue at nine. I felt at ease for the first time in weeks. No pains in my chest or head. Pain and anxiety all gone.

I checked my watch. It was just past the hour.

Nothing.

And then five minutes later all hell broke loose.

My phone started hopping on the table as call after call came through.

The phone bleeped to the continuous number of text messages that lit up the screen. I watched in amazement. I had decided to let the early calls go unanswered, but I hadn't expected such a torrent - calls which just kept coming one after the other. This continued for about ten minutes and then there was a sudden silence. I assumed that was the end, but no; my phone had just conked out. And as much as I tried, I couldn't get it going again. Perhaps this was fate.

I decided to leave my phone powered off and try to restart it again later. Barry in the Irish Press Association office had released the news at nine as agreed, and the news that we had found Ronan had clearly reached the Irish and London media.

We spent the rest of the day in the hospital with Ronan. On the way there we stopped off and bought him new nightclothes, a dressing gown and wash-things. Once he'd had a shave and changed into his new pyjamas he looked more like his old self. More like our Ronan. But he was quiet and a little downcast. I think he felt a bit embarrassed that he had ended up in a London hospital. It was clear he had no idea about the dramatic search efforts to find him at home and in London, and Martin and I were happy to play it down. It would take time for him to rehabilitate and get well.

And there'd be time enough to fill him in when we were all together at home again.

We met our friend Tanaka at Kensington South Station that evening. I was genuinely moved by his joy for us. He was so glad to hear that Ronan was in hospital and on the road to recovery, and home. I explained that we were returning to Ireland the next day and we hugged it out. He had been the first friendly face we encountered in London.

A stranger who had listened, and cared, and offered us hope and encouragement in the face of our overwhelming odds.

Once again we invited him to be our guest if he ever found himself in Ireland.

There was a little café between Kensington Station and Jury's Hotel where Martin and I had grabbed a coffee and sandwich a couple of times. We were ravenous, so we decided to stop for something to eat on our way to the hotel. The waitress knew us well by now and gave a friendly nod towards a table in the window as we came in. The notice board still held our Missing Person poster of Ronan.

Thank God we could take it down now.

The place was almost empty as we sat and ordered. I was happy just to sit there quietly. One way or another, I had been talking to anyone who would listen to me for over a month. And I was happy that I had nowhere to be. Happy to stop moving.

Just happy.

Full stop.

Suddenly the door soon burst open and a willowy young woman with flowing blonde hair and a diaphanous white dress came in and flung herself down dramatically at the far side of the room She was about twenty five to thirty years of age and stunningly beautiful. She ordered herself a coffee and my eyes were glued to her as she passed us on her way downstairs to the bathroom. Martin gave me a bit of look. But I couldn't help it. What a gorgeous girl!

We tucked into our burgers.

A few French tourists came in and the place was suddenly bustling. Five minutes went by. Then ten… When the waitress came to clear our plates, she asked if the blonde girl in the white dress had returned from the loo. When we said no, we were completely amazed at her reaction. She rolled her eyes to the heavens, threw her cloth on the table, and stomped down the stairs, leaving the café completely unattended. She reappeared a few minutes later, dragging the beautiful girl behind her and basically shoved her out the front door onto the street.

What the hell?

We were stunned. And I think I'd become highly sensitive to the idea of people being 'ejected'.

As we watched the girl, seemingly unperturbed and head held high, make her way down the busy street, the waitress returned to retrieve her cloth and our plates.

"Sorry about that."

"Yeah, it seemed a bit... I mean, what happened? Did she do something?"

"Did she *do* something? Only drives me *mad*! Comes in here nearly every day, taking up space, putting real customers off their paninis..."

"Well, I don't really..."

"Look. She pretends to order coffee, but really, she just wants to use my loo, yeah?"

"Oh, right…"

"And I'm not completely heartless, you know. I wouldn't even mind that so much. But now she comes in here to wash that stupid white dress of hers and uses my hand-dryer to dry it."

"Ah, but sure, if the poor girl's just trying to stay clean…"

"How is that my problem, though? Does this look like a launderette to you?

"No, of course not, I only…"

"Sorry. Sorry. I mean, this all puts me in a horrible position. Makes me the bad one. But I have to be tough about it. Otherwise I'd have them all in here, frightening off paying customers."

"All *who?*"

"Homeless people, you know? Yeah. There's a gang of them living in the park. Alkies and druggies, and that. Filthy, most of them. Yeah. Oh, Miss Blondie manages to keep herself clean, I'll give her that. But it's getting out of hand. They're driving all the businesses around here nuts. I'm sick of it!"

She paused, blew out a long breath, and summoned her best customer-service smile.

"Now, then. Can I get you boys anything else?"

"No. Just the bill, please."

Oh, my God!

That vision of a woman. Living on the street. It seemed impossible.

My burger settled heavily in the pit of my stomach. I looked over at Martin.

"Could you imagine if that was one of our girls?"

"No, I couldn't. Don't even go there. Anything could happen to them."

"Seriously though. That woman is completely unprotected. And so beautiful, Martin. Sleeping rough in the park? At the mercy of any old creep that came across her? It's frightening…"

"It is frightening. It is, yeah. This whole homelessness thing is…well, it's a nightmare."

"A nightmare. Yeah, you're right."

"But you'd have to wonder how she could end up like this? It's so sad. There's got to be someone out there looking for her, surely to God? Someone must be worrying about her? Missing her? I mean, she's a real person. A sister. A wife. She's old enough to be a mother, even. At the very least, she's someone's daughter. It makes you think."

We paid up and bid the waitress goodbye.

We even forgot to take down Ronan's poster.

As we made our way back to the hotel for the last night, Martin suddenly grabbed me by the arm.

"Look!"

On the far side of the busy street, beneath the red and navy archway of the Underground entrance, the beautiful café woman was clearly busking, unselfconsciously singing and swaying to the beat of a tambourine she lazily bounced between her hand and hip. We stopped to watch, both transfixed by the loveliness of her perfect face haloed in golden hair, her graceful form, and the surprisingly sultry pitch of her voice which intermittently hit us across the waves of traffic. We stood alone in our admiration.

Maybe, like Vincent, this was her regular spot and people had got used to her. In any event, the locals raced right past her, and seemingly oblivious to her or her song, disappeared into the darkness of the tunnels below.

It was a strange sensation to fall under the spell of a homeless chanteuse on the noisy urban thoroughfare. Just as we tore ourselves away, I felt her sweeping gaze come to rest on the two men openly regarding her from across the road. But if she recalled us from the café, she gave no sign of recognition. Instead she casually turned her attention to adjusting the white folds of her dress; an elegant gallantry that spared all three of us from undue embarrassment.

We left her there and walked on listlessly.

Sometimes there are no words.

But I must admit, the sadness, the *waste* of it all, was starting to wear me down.

As if reading my mind, Martin broke the silence

"Ah, look, don't take it so hard, Ciaran. I think she's tougher than she looks. And I'd say that twisted sense of humour of hers gets her through a lot."

"*Twisted* sense of humour of hers…?"

"Yeah. Didn't you hear the song she was singing?"

"She was too far away. I couldn't make it out."

"Well, *I* did…"

"And…?"

"And it was 'Material Girl' by Madonna."

Jesus!

It would be good to get home.

London had given us a parting lesson in just how cold and unforgiving the metropolis could be.

September 8th

Martin and I had arranged to fly home on Thursday evening. Then Dad and my brother Brian would fly to London on Friday evening and spend the weekend at the hospital with Ronan. My sisters Maria and Joey would follow to London a day or two later. Martin and I checked out of Jury's in the morning, crossed town to the hospital and whiled away the day with Ronan. He was settling in. The staff were attentive and supportive and we could already see an improvement.

Our temporary farewells were pretty emotional. After battling so hard to find him, it was hard to let him out of our sight. But he was safe, and Dad and the girls would be there with the next day.

So after one more round of Baxter huddles, we grabbed the Tube to Heathrow and boarded our flight to Cork.

As I took my seat on the plane, I happened to glance down. The shiny leather shoes that I had first worn when we arrived in London looked well and truly worn in. Dusty and creased. I wriggled my toes. Heels no longer sore. Yep. They were comfy now; taking on the shape of my foot.

Well, Martin and I myself had covered a fair bit of ground.

In every sense of the word.

I smiled and closed my eyes.

Thought I'd drift off for a snooze but instead my mind starting racing. For some reason my thoughts lurched to the beach scenes of Saving Private Ryan. Bit dramatic, but that's how it all felt. Brothers in arms. The search for a beloved child. I felt the sting of tears.

Deep breath…

We had been through hell. We had forced our way through brick walls. We had survived the nightmare. We were bringing Ronan home.

Alive.

The plane landed with a muffled thud. No panic to get off this time. No major rush. No *dread*.

Deep breath…

The captain announced, "Welcome to Cork. The local time is now 7.20pm."

And then, completely out of the blue,

"We would like to welcome Martin and Ciaran Baxter home, having successfully located and found their brother Ronan, who had been missing in London."

The plane broke into spontaneous yells and whoops. Gulping back tears. You've got to love the Irish.

Deep breath...

A flight attendance approached.

"Sirs, we would be delighted if you would disembark first."

Deep breath...

I scooped up my trusty laptop and holdall. No one moved from their seats and a ripple of applause broke out again as we made our way down the aisle through handclasps and back-slaps, and stepped through the open door back into the bright Cork sunshine.

Home again.

Safe and sound.

The End

Photographs - Part Two

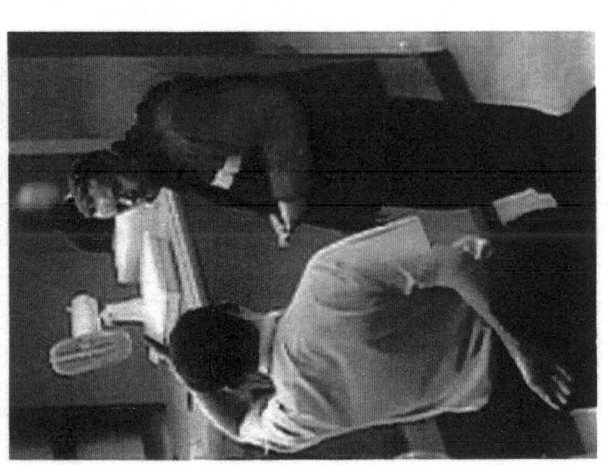

MISSING PERSON

RONAN BAXTER MISSING FROM HIS HOME

IN CORK, REP. OF IRELAND SINCE SATURDAY 13TH AUGUST

RONAN IS 5FT 11" TALL, LIGHT BROWN HAIR AND BLUE EYES. HEAVY SMOKER.

ANY INFORMATION REGARDING HIS WHEREABOUTS, PLEASE CONTACT

0208 3924510

OR

0207 2302959

Our Missing Persons poster of Ronan for UK

Ciaran Baxter

national
missing
persons
helpline

NMPH
PO Box 28908
London SW14 7ZU

Casework Dept
Tel: 020 8392 4545
Fax: 020 8878 7752

Date as postmark

Dear

Following your recent contact with us we would firstly like to reassure you that we are here to provide you with help and support. The enclosed literature explains more about the services provided by our charity and further information is available from our web site www.missingpersons.org

To enable us to assist you properly, we need you to enter the missing person's details on the enclosed form and return it to the address above as soon as possible. If you need any help in completing the forms, please ring us on 020 8392 4545 and we will be pleased to assist you.

In some situations it may be appropriate to use publicity to appeal to the public for information. In case we take up this option, we need you to sign the enclosed consent form. However, I can assure you that we would contact you again before going ahead with any publicity and then only if you agree to it.

If for any reason you decide not to return the forms, or the missing person returns, it would be very helpful if you could advise us accordingly. I trust you will understand that as a charity we always try to make efficient use of our resources so if the circumstances do change it would be appreciated if you could let us know as soon as possible.

We are here to help and support you and there is no charge for our work. But, in case you would like to make a contribution towards the work of the charity, there is a space on the back of the enclosed missing person form for you to complete if you would like to send us a donation.

Best wishes

Letter Ref:P1

Company Limited by Guarantee Incorporated in England and Wales under the Companies Act 1985. Registered no. 2614202
Co Founders: Janet Newman OBE, Mary Asprey OBE. Registered Office: 17 Hertford Avenue, London SW14 8EF

Please give generously to National Missing Persons Helpline, a charity pledged to devote its resources to supporting the families left behind and helping missing people regain contact.

Registered Charity No. 1020419

UK Missing Persons Org. letter

Bring Him Home

Ciaran Baxter

From:	"chloe.s" <chloe.s@missingpersons.org>
To:	<baxterandassociates@eircom.net>
Sent:	02 September 2005 16:08
Attach:	Ronan Baxter 2.pdf; Ronan Baxter.pdf
Subject:	Posters of Ronan

Dear Ciaran,

Here are two posters of Ronan, which may help you with your search.
Please can I ask that if you do print any out and put them up in London, please can you make a note of
where you have put them, so they can be removed and destroyed when Ronan has been found? Otherwise,
we will continue to get 'sightings'.

Thanks,

please donate online

Chloë
Case Manager

National Missing Persons
Helpline
PO Box 28908
London SW14 7ZU
United Kingdom

chloe.s@missingpersons.org
www.missingpersons.org

tel: +44 (0)20 8392 4545
fax: +44 (0)20 8878 7752

Internal Virus Database is out-of-date.
Checked by AVG Anti-Virus.
Version: 7.0.338 / Virus Database: 267.10.15/80 - Release Date: 23/08/2005

02/09/2005

UK Missing Persons Org. email

MISSING

Can you help?

Ronan Baxter
Age 39

Ronan has been missing since the 13th August 2005. He has been unwell and his family is most concerned. Any news of his whereabouts and wellbeing is desperately required.
Ronan went missing from his home in Bishopstown, Cork in Ireland; however it is known that he then travelled by plane to London.

Ronan is 5 foot 11 inches tall, is of medium build and has short brown hair. It is thought he doesn't have his glasses with him. When last seen he was wearing a jacket which was red on top with a white stripe in the middle section and navy blue in the lower section. He was wearing navy tracksuit trousers and black, casual shoes.

If you have seen Ronan or have any information as to his whereabouts, please call the confidential National Missing Persons Helpline on Freephone 0500 700 700 or email
sightings@missingpersons.org
(05-806405 cs)

Freefone
0500 700 700

National Missing Persons Helpline
www.missingpersons.org

UK Missing Persons Org. poster of Ronan

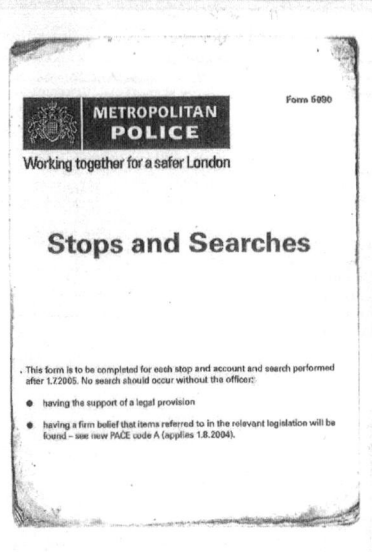

**Police Stop and Search Notice issued to Ronan in
Terminal 4, Heathrow Airport**

Police Stop and Search Notice issued to Ronan in Terminal 4, Heathrow Airport Cont.

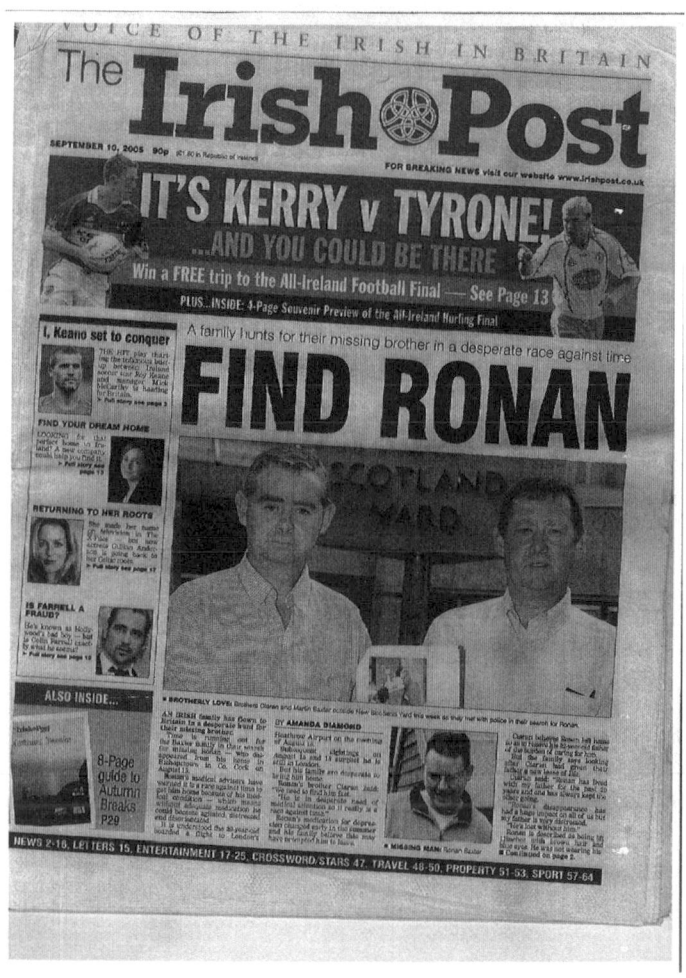

Irish Post newspaper front page appeal in UK

Form 5090

METROPOLITAN POLICE

Working together for a safer London

CHISEK POLICE Station

Stops and Searches

6/9/05

This form is to be completed for each stop and account and search performed after 1.7.2005. No search should occur without the officer:

- having the support of a legal provision

- having a firm belief that items referred to in the relevant legislation will be found – see new PACE code A (applies 1.8.2004).

Police powers to stop and search
- The law gives Police Officers powers to search you, anything you are carrying and any vehicle you are in.
- Police must use their powers of stop and search fairly and without unlawful discrimination. They will try to be considerate and courteous but they also need to be aware of their personal safety and the safety of the public.
- In some circumstances, Police Officers can use reasonable force to detain and search you.

What must a Police Officer tell you?
Before making a search, the Police Officer must take reasonable steps to tell you:
- that you are detained for the purpose of a search;
- their name (except for Anti-Terrorism searches or otherwise where the officer reasonably believes that giving their name might put them in danger, in which case their warrant number or other identification number shall be given) and the police station they are from;
- what they are searching for in general terms (the items they are looking for);
- what reason they have for searching you (excluding Terrorism powers and Powers under Section 60 Criminal Justice Act – see elsewhere in this form);
- what authority they have for searching you under Terrorism or Sec 60 CJA;
- that you are entitled to a full copy of this record now or at any time within the next 12 months.
If not in uniform they must show you their warrant card – all officers in uniform should be displaying a name badge.

How far can a Police Officer search?
- If the search takes place in public, the Police Officer can usually only ask you to remove your outer coat, jacket and gloves – except for Terrorism and Sec 60 CJA searches – see elsewhere in this form.
- Out of public view you may be asked to remove your headgear, footwear or any item concealing identity.
- If the Police Officer needs to perform a more thorough search, it must be done out of public view by a Police Officer who is the same sex as you and out of view of any person of the opposite sex to you.
Further advice may be obtained from the Metropolitan Police Internet site (at www.met.police.uk), local Citizens Advice Bureau, Metropolitan Police Authority website (at www.mpa.gov.uk) or a local community group. The Metropolitan Police is committed to increasing community confidence in its use of stops and searches.

Final Stop and Search Notice issued to Ronan at Silverhall Park, Isleworth, Hounslow, London

Final Stop and Search Notice issued to Ronan at Silverhall Park, Isleworth, Hounslow, London Cont.

Missing Cork man found safe in London

© Wed, Sep 7, 2005, 01:00

A Cork man suffering from mental health problems who disappeared after flying to London more than three weeks ago has been found safe and well, his family confirmed today.

A massive manhunt was sparked after Ronan Baxter left his father's home in Cork, where he has lived for the last 20 years, and took a flight to Heathrow Airport.

•••
The family have been overwhelmed by the level of support and assistance they have received in both Ireland and the United Kingdom, which has resulted in bringing their ordeal to a happy conclusion
A statement issued by Ciarán Baxter, brother of Ronan Baxter
Mr Baxter, 39, who suffers from severe chronic depression complicated with paranoid schizophrenia, had not been seen since August 20, when he was spotted in the Bayswater area of west London.

His family feared his condition was rapidly deteriorating as he had no medication with him.

His brother, Ciarán Baxter, travelled to the city last weekend to meet Inspector Rave Pillai of the Metropolitan Police's missing persons bureau as part of efforts to locate him.

Mr Baxter today issued a statement confirming Ronan had been found in London and was now safe and receiving the appropriate medical care.

"His family wish to thank the gardaí, the Metropolitan Police, the public, the media and the various organisations for all their help during the past weeks," he said.

"The family have been overwhelmed by the level of support and assistance they have received in both Ireland and the United Kingdom, which has resulted in bringing their ordeal to a happy conclusion.

"Ronan's father now asks that the media respect the need for privacy so as to ensure Ronan's well-being and return to ful health." A huge search was launched in Ireland after Ronan went missing on August 13.

Following appeals through the media at home and in Britain it emerged he had boarded a flight to London. His family said he had been extremely unwell earlier this year, and was admitted to Cork University Hospital for treatment.

Press Statement UK and Ireland

About the Author

I am one of a large family of seven who was born and reared in the family home in Bishopstown, Cork. My mother died of cancer in December 1980 at the age of forty eight and her death left a big mark on all our lives. I attended school in Colaiste an Spioraid Naoimh, Bishopstown, Cork and afterwards I completed a Bachelor of Arts degree in University College Cork. After college I went on to work as a trainee accountant in Cork city and in 1983 I completed my accountancy exams, having being awarded first place in Ireland in my professional stage exams.

In the same year, 1983, I started my own accountancy and tax advisory practice in Cork, Baxter & Associates, and thankfully through hard work, long hours and with some good fortune, the business grew and expanded. Partly due to the long hours of work and due to other related factors, in January 2013 I suffered a heart attack which resulted in an emergency heart operation that gave me a much needed wake-up call. As a result, in March 2016 I merged my practice with another firm and I have since been able to take a little more time out to concentrate on finishing this publication.

I am married to Sally and we have three children, Jamie, Lisa and Kayleigh.

This is the first book that I have written and while it has taken many years to finish, the story is timeless.